A FLY TYER'S GUIDE TO
FISHING
FLIES

A FLY TYER'S GUIDE TO
FISHING FLIES

Includes step-by-step instructions for tying and identifying over 100 of the most successful fishing flies, with information on all the materials and tools needed

A complete fly selector with expert advice on choosing and using the right fly for every situation, shown in more than 250 vibrant photographs and illustrations

MARTIN FORD

LB

This edition is published by Lorenz Books
an imprint of Anness Publishing Ltd
info@anness.com
www.lorenzbooks.com
www.annesspublishing.com

© Anness Publishing Ltd 2024

If you like the images in this book and would like to investigate using
them for publishing, promotions or advertising, please visit our website
www.practicalpictures.com for more information.

Publisher: Joanna Lorenz
Editor: Daniel Hurst
Designer: Simon Daley
Photography: Paul Bricknell and Martin Ford
Indexer: Ann Barrett
Production: Ben Worley

A CIP catalogue record for this book is available from the British Library.

PUBLISHER'S NOTE

CONTENTS

6 Introduction

8 TOOLS, MATERIALS AND HOOKS
10 Fly-Tying Materials
14 Tools for the Fly tyer
18 Hooks used in Fly Tying

20 FLY-TYING TECHNIQUES
22 Fixing the Hook in the Vice
22 Tying On
23 The Whip Finish
23 The Whip-finish Tool
24 Tying a Tail
24 Dubbing
25 Tying a Hackle
25 Tying Wings
26 Adams Dry Fly
27 Silver Invicta
28 Cat's Whisker
29 Fuzzy Buzzer
30 Pheasant Tail Nymph

31 Deer Hair Fry
32 Hotspot Leaded Shrimp Fly
33 Salmon Shrimp Fly
34 Garry Dog
35 Olive Goldhead
36 Knots

40 A DIRECTORY OF FISHING FLIES
42 Dry Flies
54 Wet Flies
66 Salmon & Sea Trout Flies
   68 Salmon Flies
   71 Sea Trout Flies
74 Lures
82 Nymphs & Buzzers
   84 Nymphs
   89 Fishing with Buzzers
   92 Buzzers

94 Glossary
95 Index and Acknowledgements

INTRODUCTION

Fly fishing is a skilful art, one where man can pit his wits against nature, and at the same time, be at one with the world around him. Though the techniques can be taught, most anglers spend a lifetime learning how to read the water, how to understand the quarry and know when to strike. Every fishing expedition is different and, since the environment changes hourly, the flies that catch the choicest fish on one occasion may not at the next.

BELOW *A solitary fly fisher patiently waiting for a bite. Hand-tying fishing flies can be time consuming, but to catch a fish on a fly that you have tied yourself is a great achievement.*

The practice of tying flies has been passed on through generations of fly-fishing folk, fly fishers who, through centuries of practice, have strived to imitate the natural food of their chosen quarry. Once you have successfully mastered the art of fly fishing you too will more than likely feel the urge to start tying your own patterns of fishing flies. There's nothing quite like dispatching a salmon or trout that has just fallen for a pattern of fly that has been lovingly tied by your very own hands.

Although seen as an accomplished art, for the beginner, tying your own flies brings a whole new dimension to the sport of fly fishing, which with practice can become an extremely satisfying pastime.

In this day and age there is an abundance of information on the internet and within the pages of books on fly tying to be able to confidently 'self-teach' the basic craft. As a beginner to fly tying, and armed with all manner of feather, fur and hook

HOW THIS BOOK WORKS

This book is divided into several different sections, giving you a complete insight into the wonderful world of fly tying.

The opening section looks at the armoury of materials, tools and hooks that the fly tyer has available to them. It is here that the fledgling fly tyer will learn the uses of the many different tying materials available, and exactly which tools are essential when starting out. Uses for furs, feathers and many synthetic materials are all covered, with suggestions as to their use within the realms of already established fly patterns. The different sizes and shapes of hooks are also explained, so that you can grasp which to use, and when.

Moving on from this, the following section examines some of the techniques used by the avid fly tyer. These are demonstrated in easy-to-follow step-by-step photographic sequences that will help you to truly master the techniques needed to construct your own flies. After these basic techniques there are further sequences that allow you tie complete flies from scratch – these work through every major fly type from wet and dry flies, to nymphs and buzzers. This section closes with a look at some of the knots available to the fly tyer, so that you can be sure never to lose your carefully crafted fly once it is on the line.

The second half of the book is a directory of classic fishing flies that is split into subsections on dry flies, wet flies, salmon flies, sea trout flies, lures, nymphs and buzzers. Each entry includes a fascinating history of each fly, plus key information on how and when to use it. There are also full materials listings for every pattern, so that you can attempt to create any fly featured in the book using the practical skills that you learn in the techniques section.

The book closes with a glossary of fly-fishing terms that should leave you fully prepared to use the skills you have learned to create your own flies. With a creative mind and the right materials there is no limit to what the fly tyer can craft at the tying vice. Fly tying is an art that will mature with you and give hours of pleasure, both at the work bench and out on the bank in pursuit of your quarry.

LEFT A selection of fully dressed fishing flies. The variety of colours and textures used to create these flies truly make them miniature works of art.

patterns, you can spend hours honing your skills until you are completely happy with a fly pattern that's been imitated from a book, or indeed, for the more adventurous among you, a pattern that you have devised yourself.

Although there are thousands of historically established patterns, one of the great joys of fly tying is the ability to experiment, especially as more and more new materials become available.

You may well want to enrol in a fly-tying class and learn from a professional fly-tying expert. Fly-fishing associations, and even colleges, now offer evening or weekend courses for the budding tyer, where the learning curve can be extremely rapid, allowing you to master the art of tying at a quicker pace than the self-taught route can provide.

Your first patterns will inevitably look clumsy, but as time passes and you start to grasp the techniques, the process will start to feel a lot more natural and the results will be more impressive.

For beginners through to the more advanced, the internet and indeed the local fly-fishing tackle shop can provide all manner of materials and tools to suit the level of creative fly tying that you find yourself at. Choose wisely when making your purchases and don't be tempted into buying expensive equipment if you don't really need it. It's better to start off with the basic equipment, perhaps in the form of a starter kit, and then upgrade or add to it when you have established yourself as a keen fly tyer.

Do seek the advice of others around you, especially those with more knowledge and those who share your passion for fly tying. Not only will you pick up some good tying tips, but you may also learn about materials or patterns of flies that are successful yet relatively easy to tie.

TOOLS, MATERIALS AND HOOKS

This opening section explores the tools, materials and hooks that are available to the fly tyer. Using these three components the fly fisher attempts to create a device that will deceive and entice any fish that comes across it.

The section opens by looking at the plethora of materials that can be used to create a fishing fly. From natural components such as brightly coloured feathers and luxuriant furs, through to modern, synthetic materials including shiny tinsels and colourful beads. It is from this vibrant armoury that the fly tyer selects the core substances of their fishing fly when planning a new design, carefully crafting them to emulate combinations of colour, shape and texture that are actually found in nature.

Following this we examine the tools available to the fly tyer. It is important that the tyer has access to some essential items, with the most crucial tool being a trusty vice. Advice on what to look for when choosing a vice, and other tools, is given, as well as information on the purpose of each tool and how to use it effectively.

The section closes by looking at some of the hooks that can be used when fly tying. Hooks determine the size and weight of the flies, so it is essential that the tyer understands their uses and how to use them effectively.

FLY-TYING MATERIALS

A wide array of materials are utilized in the construction of fishing flies. Natural furs, feathers and fibres lend themselves brilliantly to creating beautiful and convincing flies, but modern-day fly tyers also have a host of artificial, synthetic materials available to them from beyond nature's bounty, making the choice of materials almost endless.

BELOW A well-equipped fly tyer's desk with an exciting array of materials. The vast range of colours and textures available to the tyer means that it is possible to convincingly imitate almost anything found in nature.

The list of materials currently in use by the modern-day fly tyer is virtually never-ending. There are literally thousands of both natural and synthetic materials that can be utilized in the manufacturing of fishing flies. As you move from beginner to intermediate ability and your tying skills progress, the desire to experiment will lead you to try many new and varied materials. Sourcing can be fun and can lead you to finding all manner of new materials and ideas that can be used in the construction of fishing flies, and there is no greater reward than catching a fish on a fly that you have lovingly designed and constructed yourself.

The most commonly and historically used materials are from a natural source, such as bird feathers and animal skins. But in recent years the inclusion of manufactured fibres to replace, or complement, natural materials has become more common. When purchasing fly-tying materials it is important to ensure that they are of a high quality, as this will reflect in your finished flies; to guarantee this, always buy from a reputable retailer or dealer. The internet is fast becoming a very reliable source for new materials, particularly where price is an issue, and it is far easier now to purchase fly-tying materials from all over the world.

For the beginner, an afternoon spent in the company of an experienced fly tyer is a good way of seeking advice in selecting the right type of materials and is also an invaluable aid to learning the correct way to construct certain patterns of fly. Fly-fishing clubs often have a resident fly-tying professional who will either coach on a one-to-one basis for a small fee, or give group tuition at club meetings. If you don't belong to a club there is a worldwide network of fly tyers that can be found via the internet, and a few lessons in tying at the early stages of your fly-tying career will stand you in good stead for the future.

When it comes to choosing the patterns you would like to make, ensure that you buy the relevant material and try to master one or two simple patterns before moving on to something that requires a more skilful hand. It is far easier to master the tying of simple patterns, and the practice will aid your ability for more complex flies.

If you have access to a local game shoot, it is worth approaching a member, as they may be able to supply you with an assortment of game-bird feathers and even furs. This is far less expensive than having to import smaller quantities from far off destinations. Next time you visit the zoo, remember to ask the keepers to save you any of the brightly coloured discarded feathers from the tropical birds they keep. For the opportunist fly tyer, the death of a pheasant on the roadside is a gift as there is a use for much of this bird's plumage at the fly tyer's vice. Also, look around your home and consider using unlikely materials such as the discarded fur from a groomed pet or even synthetic materials from modern-day life, such as a chenille scarf or even foam packaging. Finally, and above all, when tying a known pattern or indeed trying to create something from your own findings, take your time and don't rush.

Fly tying is a form of art – the process should be enjoyed and the end product will represent the time and effort that you have put into it. When you first start tying flies it may be useful to remember that what you are trying to create is a 'silhouette trigger', meaning that the fly's outline should trigger a response in the fish that you are trying to catch. The size, shape, colour and movement of a fly in the water will all contribute to this illusion and should all be taken into consideration when planning a new design.

When it comes to purchasing the actual materials that are required for each pattern of fly that you wish to tie, you will find that they are often listed within different categories. Different parts of a bird or animal will have several different uses in fly tying as will the modern-day synthetic materials, so it is important to be aware of how each material can be used.

Most good retailers or online stores will list their products within these self-explanatory categories, making selection far easier. For the total beginner to the art of fly tying, it might be a better option to purchase a starter kit. Most good-quality starter kits come with a selection of the appropriate tools and a sufficient selection of tying materials, such as feathers, furs and threads. They usually come with a proper instruction booklet and a guide on how to tie a few of the more common patterns.

For those that are ready to embark on a life long journey as a fly tyer however, individual purchases of materials are probably better. Do think about storage for all the items that you are likely to buy. Feathers, for example, are likely to get damaged if left out on your tying bench, so good-quality transparent tubes or airtight plastic envelopes are a good option. You might even want to invest in a fly tyer's box for all your sundry items.

ABOVE *It is important to store all of your fly-tying materials carefully. Threads and tinsels can get tangled, and feathers are easily damaged if they are left out. A small, compartmentalized storage container, such as the one above, is a good option for the fledgling fly tyer.*

RIGHT *A selection of dyed and natural furs. Fur can either be bought attached to a section of treated animal skin or as finely chopped up dubbing, which is used to form the bodies of many fly patterns.*

FEATHERS

All manner of birds' feathers are used within fly tying, and feathers as a whole can be split into several categories, such as 'wings', 'tails' and 'capes'. Wings could come from a number of different breeds of wild birds, and the fly tyer may require wings from species such as coot, grouse, cock pheasant and teal duck. Capes are another feather item, and Indian cock capes are commonly sold for tying purposes.

Tail feathers from pheasants and peacocks are widely used, as are single or bunches of feathers from ducks, partridges, ostriches and even turkeys, which provide fine marabou. This downy feather comes from a domestic turkey and is available in plain white plus a whole range of dyed colours, including fluorescents; however, white, black and olive are the most popular.

The texture of the marabou gives it a superb pulsing action and it is used widely in tying reservoir lures and tadpoles. Another widely used feather is a cock hackle, which comes from the neck of a domestic chicken and is used for tails, wings and, most commonly, for the hackles of wet and dry flies. Cock hackles come in a wide range of natural and dyed colours.

These are only a few examples of feathers, and as you progress you will come across all manner of exotic bird feathers from all over the world.

FEATHER FIBRE

Many types of feather, such as pheasant tail and ostrich and goose quills, are used either plain or dyed to create soft, natural-looking bodies in a variety of nymph and dry-fly patterns. Sections of wing quills from either the mallard duck or starling are also used for the wings of wet and dry flies.

FURS

When we talk of furs we are referring to animal furs, and different patterns of fly historically demand certain types of fur for construction. Furs from squirrels, deer, foxes and elk are commonly used to make flies, but the fur of any animal could be used. When you purchase fur you will receive a section of dried and treated animal skin which has the fur still intact; small amounts can then be cut from the patch using sharp scissors.

DUBBING

Many furs, such as hare, rabbit and seal, are used for dubbing – which is the use of fine fibres to create the body of a fly. Furs come in a vast range of natural, dyed colours and may be used for wet flies, dry flies and nymphs. Manmade products, such as Antron and polypropylene, are also widely used.

BELOW *A selection of feather capes. The striking plumage of grouse and pheasant make them excellent fly-tying materials. Feathers are also dyed in vivid colours for more exotic flies.*

TYING THREAD

This is the fine, strong thread that holds together the materials used to construct the fly. Originally natural silk was used, but today manmade rot-proof products such as nylon are the most popular. Tying thread now comes in a wide range of colours and thicknesses, although black, brown and olive are the most commonly used. Most threads are waxed, which gives additional grip and protection for tying. Threads can also be used to build up the body and head sections of a fly. Once the fly has been completed, the head section (where the thread will usually end) is covered in varnish to further protect it.

TINSEL

Providing flies with a vibrant sparkle that catches the light and helps to attract fish up from the murky depths, tinsel comes either in a flat strip, as a spooled round thread or as a wire. Once metal, tinsels are now either coated or made from plastics to prevent them from tarnishing. Silver and gold are the traditional colours but pearl lurex and even bright reds and yellows are very popular in modern patterns. Tinsel's primary use in constructing flies is for creating body sections or for ribbing a body section, particularly on lures and salmon flies. Tinsel is available in different thicknesses depending on its intended use.

FLOSS

Available in a wide range of colours, floss is normally wound along a hook to create a slim, tapered body. Silk was the original material but rayon, which winds flat and smooth, is very popular today. Recently, stretchable products have become more widely used.

WOOL

With its coarse texture, wool is ideal for winding or for teasing out and dubbing on to create a chunky body. It can also be used for tails. Wool comes in a wide range of colours, both plain and fluorescent.

CHENILLE

French for 'caterpillar', chenille certainly has a worm-like appearance and is usually wound along the hook to create a dense, succulent body. It comes in a range of colours and diameters, and can be used for lures right down to small nymphs.

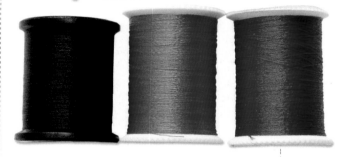

SYNTHETICS

There are hundreds of different synthetic materials now available, but one of the more common ones is mylar, which is a form of manmade tinsel. This is primarily used for the construction of the body section of a fly, such as a lure. Foams of all different colours can be used to create bodies, heads and even eyes for some of the bigger lure flies.

Products such as flashabou and frizz fibre also have their uses when it comes to tying in tail sections, again particularly on reservoir lures. Other items that you will come across are 'eyes', which are normally formed from small beads or sections of chain. Silicone rubber also has a place in the fly tyer's box, and there are many different colours to choose from.

Weighted beads, made either from brass or tungsten are another must. They are usually used for the construction of a weighted head, particularly on lures that are fished down in the water. Beyond the synthetics mentioned above, there is a myriad of materials at the fly tyer's disposal, and although historic patterns will require a disciplined approach with the appropriate materials, when it comes to creating something new, it really is down to the limits of your own imagination.

TOOLS FOR THE FLY TYER

The minute scale of many fishing flies makes fly tying a very skilled art. The use of tools, such as a sturdy vice or precise pliers, instead of clumsy fingers, makes it possible to make delicate adjustments when constructing a pattern, and to craft some very accurate, and truly beautiful flies. There is a wide range of tools to choose from, but a reliable vice will give you a solid base from which to start.

For many experienced fly fishers, the inherent enjoyment of tying their own flies and catching fish on patterns that they themselves have tied go hand in hand. Even for the novice, with a little practice and a bit of practical advice, the ability to tie simple but effective flies is only a short time away. As your enthusiasm for fly fishing progresses it is only right that you'll want to learn to tie flies yourself to further heighten the thrill of landing a fish.

For those about to embark upon tying their own patterns of flies, the first step is to select the right equipment, and most good tackle shops can offer advice on selecting the tools that you are likely to need. Some of the larger tools, such as the vice, can be expensive but are nevertheless vital for the fledgling fly tyer.

Before you make your selection of tools and vice, do think about where you are going to tie your flies. Most professionals have a special bench or a worktop, a place where their tying vice is permanently fixed in position with easy access to all the tools and materials that they are likely to need. If you are confined to the garden shed, do ensure that all the materials like feathers and fur are stored in airtight containers to protect them from any possible dampness. Think about the size of the working area you will require, and also think about the storage facilities for tools and materials. Lighting should also be considered, as poor light will result in you straining your eyes and possibly losing consistency within the patterns that you are attempting to tie.

BELOW It is important to have a dedicated area for fly tying. Having your vice firmly secured to a worktop and your tools and materials readily available means that you can be ready to embark on tying a new pattern almost immediately.

At the head of the vice are its jaws, usually constructed from hardened steel, and it is the jaw section that grips the hook firmly in place, allowing the tyer enough room to apply all of the various materials around the hook.

When choosing a vice it is vital to ensure that the jaws really can grip both large and small hooks securely. Many models of vice will have a further adjustment on the jaws to allow this type of precision grip. Rather than choosing the cheapest vice, try to budget for something a little higher in price – after all, the vice is an essential tool and the right choice of vice should last you for quite a few years. If you do buy a cheap model and you really take to fly tying, then you will probably be back at the tackle shop within a few months to upgrade to a better, more expensive model.

Most fly-tying vices will be lever-operated. This allows the tyer to exert the right amount of pressure by depressing a cammed lever to the rear of the vice, so that the hook can be secured in place between the jaws. Modern-day models feature precision jaws and in some cases a 360-degree rotating head, allowing the tyer access to all sides of the pattern of fly that they are tying, without having to manually turn the hook around.

Upmarket vices can feature an over-vice light, for those intricate details in tying, and some feature a magnifying glass. The magnifying glass is usually fitted on a flexible arm that fixes on to the body of the vice when it's required.

Finding the right vice for your needs can be a time-consuming process, as it is important to test as many as possible before making a decision. When properly researched it can be a tool that lasts a lifetime, so weigh up your own personal needs and consider factors such as ease of use, weight and hook access to narrow down your selection. Ultimately though, it is important to find a vice that feels right for you.

LEFT The vice is an essential tool for fly tying. The hook is clamped firmly into position allowing the tyer to construct the fly.

For those with limited space there is an array of small tying cabinets available, specially crafted with drawers to store all of your materials in. Most fly-fishing tackle companies now also produce purpose-built fly-tying luggage, where all your materials, tools and even a vice can be kept. These storage solutions not only look smart, but also protect your valuable materials and, when properly ordered, make sure that you have all of your materials, tools and equipment to hand at a moment's notice.

VICE

The most important tool of all is the fly tyer's vice, for without it you will struggle to secure a hook on to which your materials will be tied. The vice will either fit on to the tying bench by way of a clamp at its base, or have a heavy enough base to become freestanding.

A freestanding model does offer far more versatility, especially if you want to take the vice away with you on holiday or indeed on fly-fishing trips, where you might want to tie custom patterns to suit the water and conditions that you are fishing at the time.

LEFT This vice is designed to clamp on to a work surface, but freestanding models are available. It is possible to secure your vice with additional clamps, such as the one pictured here.

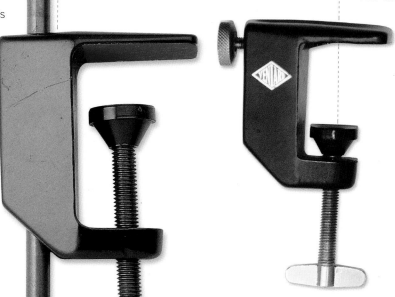

RIGHT *Scissors,
dubbing needles and a
hackle guard – all vital
components of the keen
fly-tyer's toolbox.*

SCISSORS

At least one pair of sharp fine-pointed scissors is needed to prepare materials and to trim off any excess or wayward fibres when in the process of tying. Some tyers prefer curved blades, but whichever you choose do ensure they are very sharp. Surgical scissors will meet this requirement if you can obtain them. It is better to have two pairs, as one can be used for cutting and trimming delicate fur, hackles and feathers, while the second pair should be more robust and will mainly be used for tinsel, fine wires or other tough materials.

HACKLE PLIERS

This small sprung-wire tool grips hackles and other fine materials between its jaws, allowing them to be wound easily without being damaged by the fingers. Make sure that the hackle pliers you choose have rubber-covered jaws to prevent them cutting or crushing delicate hackle fibres. As with scissors, it is advisable to obtain two pairs, as they can be very easily misplaced.

BOBBIN HOLDER

The bobbin holder helps the tyer apply the tying thread, while keeping waste to a minimum. It also provides additional weight, which allows the thread to be left hanging from the part-tied pattern of fly, while still retaining enough tension to stop any of the materials falling away. Always choose a spigot bobbin holder, preferably one with a ceramic tube. The ceramic is extremely hard and smooth, and never damages fine thread, unlike the old-fashioned metal ones. You don't have to limit yourself to just one bobbin holder either. If you do, then you'll have to keep swapping the different threads over each time you require them. Most professionals keep at least three bobbin holders with pre-selected coloured threads on them.

WHIP-FINISH TOOL

With its sprung metal arms, the whip-finish tool is a great help to those who find the task of whip finishing – completing a fly – difficult using the fingers.

DUBBING NEEDLE

This simple little tool is used for teasing out fine dubbing materials, freeing any trapped fibres, hairs or feathers. It can also be used for applying varnish to a finished pattern.

RIGHT *Hackle pliers.
These handy tools grip
the hackle, which
represents the fly's legs,
and other fine materials
in their vice-like jaws.*

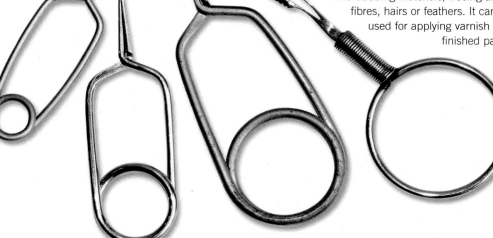

HACKLE GUARD

Though it is not an essential tool when you first start tying flies, a hackle guard will aid the finishing of a pattern as your tying skill starts to improve, especially when you get to the stage of whip finishing (applying the last of the thread at a forward point of the hackle). The hackle guard is designed to hold back the hackle fibres so that they do not get trapped underneath the finishing thread, which could potentially ruin the shape of the completed fly.

WING SELECTORS

This a small tool that comes in handy for the selection of wing material, especially when sizing wings. When tying more than one fly of a set pattern and of the same size, the wing selector will ensure an equal size of wing for each separate fly.

There are many other tying tools and labour-saving devices that you might well come across as your tying progresses. However, the ones discussed here are the essential ones, which should provide you with all of the assistance you will need to tie most patterns of fishing fly effectively.

ABOVE *A bobbin holder. Having several bobbin holders on standby, each loaded with a different colour thread, is an efficient approach to fly tying.*

LEFT *A whip-finish tool and dubbing needle set. The whip-finish tool allows the fly tyer to finish tying a fly quickly and neatly – this can be accomplished with the fingers but many find using a tool much easier.*

HOOKS USED IN FLY TYING

The fishing fly is the archetypal wolf in sheep's clothing. Beneath its cunning disguise of delicate feathers, colourful fur and shiny tinsel, lies its true form – the barbarous hook. There are many different types of hook available to the fly tyer, and choosing the right one for each pattern that you tie is essential, as the size and weight of a hook will help to determine at what depth a fly will sit in the water.

BELOW *Beneath its showy costume the hook forms the basis for many fishing flies. The fly tyer's task is to take the simple hook and make it look irresistible to their prey.*

Hooks form the base of many fly patterns and are available in various shapes, weights, sizes and wire gauges. There are literally thousands of different brands and hundreds of patterns to choose from, so choosing the right one can be a daunting task for the fledgling fly tyer. Some are shaped to imitate the body shape of the natural insect, which can make achieving a convincing silhouette slightly easier, while other less-specialized hooks can be used as the base for a wide variety of different patterns.

The size of a hook and gauge of wire help determine which pattern of fly is tied on to it. For example a light wire hook is ideal for a pattern of fly presented on, or near, the surface of the water, and a heavy wire hook is perfect for fishing a fly at greater depth. Most good retailers of fly-tying hooks will have a full catalogue listing of patterns with a description of what the hook is best suited for.

For the novice fly tyer it is probably best to keep things simple to start off with and stick to either wet fly hooks or dry fly hooks and progress from there. Listed on the opposite page are a few examples of hooks and their uses. These are only a small handful of the many patterns available, but they are among the most useful and commonly used.

SALMON SINGLE HOOK This hook is used for dressing salmon flies. It has a distinctive upturned eye, which lends itself to the turle knot used to connect the fly to the leader. The knot holds the fly upright. It grips the fly from behind the eye, allowing no flexibility where the knot meets the hook. Due to the size of salmon as a species the hook is often a large hook and sizes can range from size 4 up to 10.

STREAMER HOOK The streamer (or lure) hook is widely used for tying fry imitations and large attractor patterns such as lures. It has an elongated shank and is made from heavy-gauge wire, making it the most suitable choice for larger patterns of fly that are fished below the surface of the water.

NYMPH HOOK This hook has a long shank that is essential for imitating the long bodies of the natural insect at larvae stage. The gauge of wire varies depending upon the depth at which the fly is to be fished. A tight coil of lead wire can be wound down the shank to give additional weight. Again, this is a pattern used below the surface.

MAYFLY HOOK Designed to imitate the shape of a mayfly in its natural state. The longer shank of this hook aids the construction of the long body needed to represent this fly accurately. It is made from a medium-gauge wire and is buoyant, which allows it to float on the surface of the water, as a mayfly would.

SPROAT HOOK Used for the production of wet fly patterns. Used for attractor, traditional and imitative patterns, it is fished below the surface. It is a down-eyed pattern made from heavy gauge wire. A popular choice for beaded flies, it can also be used for sea trout, trout and grayling flies.

SEDGE HOOK The sedge hook is constructed from a heavy gauge of wire. It has a wide gap between the hook point and shank. It is used for dressing curved and bulky-bodied flies and is an ideal subject for adding to a lead underbody. This hook was originally designed for tying sedge pupae imitations, but it is also very good for tying shrimp flies.

GRUB HOOK Used in tying curved-bodied imitations that are fished below the surface of the water. It is a popular choice for tying grayling bugs, when used in small sizes, and for imitating buzzer patterns. The wire is strong and heavy.

DOWN-EYED DRY FLY HOOK This fine wire hook is used for constructing buoyant dry flies. It requires minimal dressing with fine materials. Most commonly used in sizes 10–18. It is suitable for use on both river and still water patterns of dry flies.

UP-EYED DRY FLY HOOK This well-established pattern is of a fine- to medium-gauge wire and is commonly used to imitate adult natural insects. The majority of patterns tied on this hook will be of an up-wing and heavily hackled design. This makes the fly very buoyant.

MIDGE HOOK Produced in small sizes and used for the imitation of minute insects found on or near the surface of the water. It is of a very fine wire gauge, allowing minimal use of materials to keep it afloat. When the trout are on the surface feeding on minuscule life forms, this is the perfect hook to use.

LEFT *A selection of classic hooks that are used to tie fishing flies.*

BELOW *The impressive 'Jay P.T.' fishing fly, which is tied using a salmon single hook.*

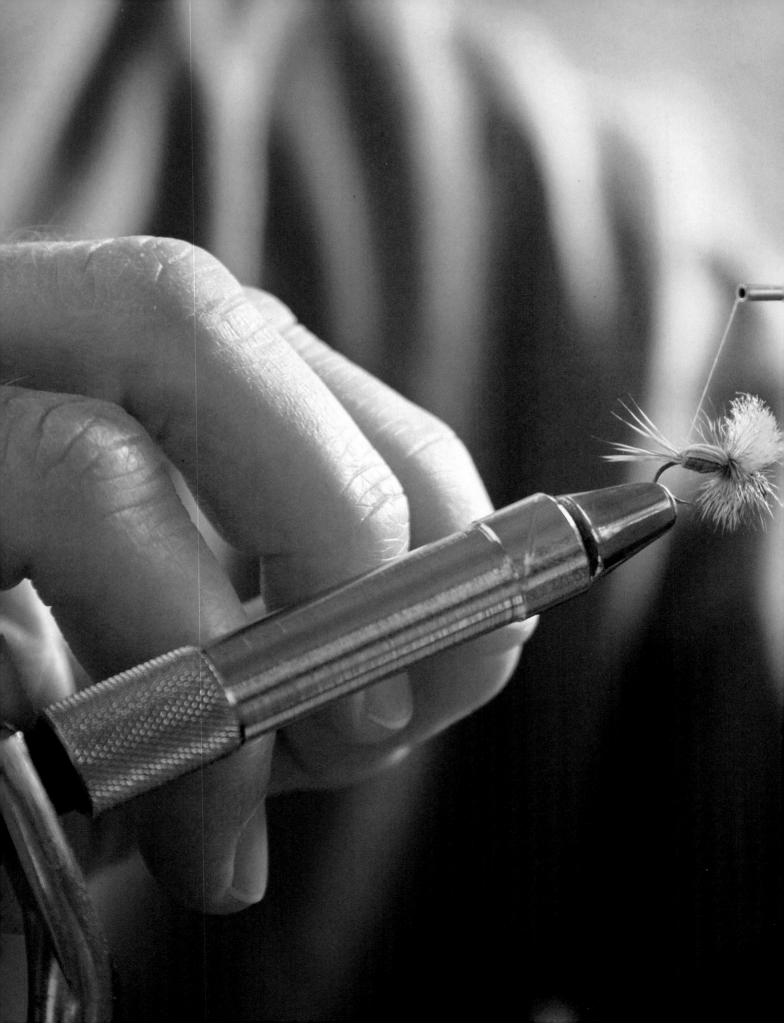

FLY-TYING TECHNIQUES

This section looks at some of the most important techniques that a fly tyer can learn. Once you have these basics mastered you will be ready to start tying your own patterns from scratch, first of all following set patterns, but eventually using your own designs and initiative to create truly unique flies.

The techniques that are covered here include fixing the hook into the vice, tying the thread on to the hook, and the whip finish – which can be achieved either by hand or using a handy tool.

More advanced methods that are explored include tying a tail, adding dubbing to a fly, tying a hackle and tying wings. These techniques can be adapted and used to tie any fly that you want to produce – so it is important that you spend time learning them before embarking on tying your own flies.

After mastering these practices you will be ready to tie your first complete fly. This section closes with practical step-by-step sequences that will allow you to create beautiful fishing flies from scratch. There are examples of all the key types of fly – from wet and dry flies, to nymphs and buzzers and also a close look at the knots that are needed to tie them. Each is presented with easy-to-follow instructions and clear photographs that will allow you to develop your skills and become a truly competent fly tyer.

FIXING THE HOOK IN THE VICE

The first step when tying a fly is to fix the hook in the vice. The object is to secure the hook so that it doesn't move as you wind the thread, leaving enough of it showing to allow easy application of the materials. Most fly-tying vices have jaws where the gap can be altered by turning a knurled wheel just in front of the

lever. To fix the hook, insert the bend of the hook in the jaws and depress the lever firmly. If after depressing the lever fully the hook is still loose, turn the wheel so that the gap decreases slightly. Adjust the gap a little at a time until it is small enough so that the jaws grip the hook firmly when the lever is fully depressed.

1 Offer the hook up to the jaws and see if it fits, so that the hook is held firmly in the vice.

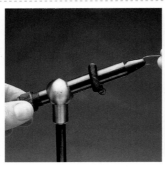

2 If the gap is incorrect adjust the jaws with the knurled wheel until it is slightly greater than the thickness of the hook.

3 Depress the lever fully to grip the hook firmly. If it is necessary you can loosen the jaws slightly to adjust the hook's position.

4 Ensure that the shank of the hook is horizontal and only the bend is masked. You can then apply the materials more easily.

TYING ON

With the hook fixed firmly in the vice and in the correct position, it is time to apply the tying thread. Tying thread is used to hold all the other materials in place, so it is the first thing to be fixed to the hook. It is normally run on at the hook's eye and then taken down the shank and secured at the tail of the fly.

The method is to loop the tying thread over the shank and wind the other end of the thread over it and the hook shank. This puts the thread under friction and secures the loose end in place. To help illustrate the correct procedure, thicker floss, which is more visible, rather than tying thread, has been used.

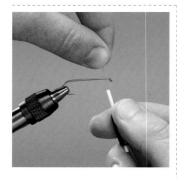

1 Offer up the thread behind the shank of the hook and near to the eye. Bring the bobbin forward over the hook, keeping the thread taut.

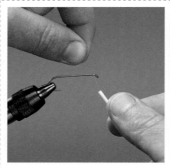

2 Holding the thread taut using a bobbin holder, wind the thread down the shank so that it covers the loose end. Five or six turns will be enough.

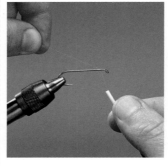

3 Repeat this process towards the bend of the hook in neat touching turns.

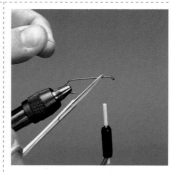

4 Trim the trapped tail to complete tying on.

THE WHIP FINISH

With the tying thread in place you are now almost ready to tie a fly. But first you must learn how to finish off. It may sound back to front but without learning how to finish off a fly securely all your efforts will be wasted – your creation will simply fall to bits when being cast.

At the end of the process, when the dressed fly is ready to be finished, the thread should be at the eye of the hook. The sequence that is laid out below shows how to make a hand whip finish. As an alternative, a whip-finish tool can be used to achieve the same effect (see bottom half of this page).

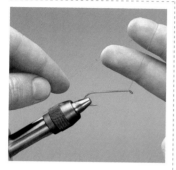

1 With the bobbin in the left hand, wrap the thread over the forefinger and middle finger of the right hand.

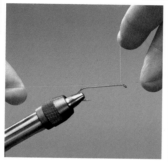

2 Catch the thread behind the middle finger and form a loop above the hook shank, keeping the thread tight.

3 Twist the fingers holding the loop around the hook shank, trapping the bobbin thread. Repeat this movement towards the eye of the hook.

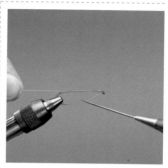

4 Using a dubbing needle, close down the loop fully by pulling on the bobbin thread. Trim off the waste thread and varnish the fly finish.

THE WHIP-FINISH TOOL

In the sequence below a tool has been used to create the whip finish. The whip-finish tool is a very handy and relatively inexpensive labour-saving device, so is a must for all but the most purist of fly tyers. Using a tool is the most commonly employed method for tying this finish, and is especially useful for novices –

although many of the most experienced fly tyers are reliant on this useful gadget.

The whip finish is normally made once all the materials have been added and a small head formed. However, for ease of illustration this sequence uses a bare hook and floss, rather than normal tying thread.

1 Assuming the fly has been completed, take hold of the tying thread and loop it over both hooks of the whip-finishing tool so that it makes a triangle.

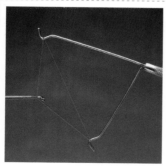

2 Flip the tool over, this will form one turn of the whip finish. Repeat the process five times adding an extra turn over the loose end every time.

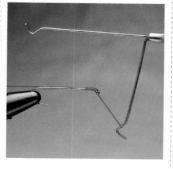

3 When the turns have been completed flip the thread off the top hook and, keeping tension with the lower hook, pull the loose end of thread.

4 Remove the lower hook and pull the thread tight. The head of the fly can now be varnished to prevent the thread wearing.

TYING A TAIL

Tails can take on an imitative or attractor role. Materials for the imitative fly tail include golden pheasant crest or tippets, pheasant tail, hackle fibres, squirrel tail, bucktail and deer hair among others. The material that you use will depend on the pattern that you are tying, as some materials offer a much

more delicate finish than others. For an attractor pattern, use materials such as marabou and a wide variety of flosses, as these will produce a large tail with lots of movement to attract the fish. The sequence below demonstrates the basic method for tying a tail, regardless of the material that you choose.

1 Tie on a neat foundation of thread along the shank of the hook to the bend. Offer up the selected material at the bend of the hook.

2 Position the material on top of the shank and catch it in with a tight turn of bobbin thread. Keep the material uniform and straight.

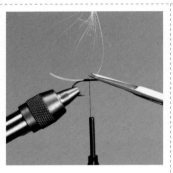

3 Take the bobbin thread in neat, touching turns back towards the eye, forming enough turns to secure the material. Trim any waste.

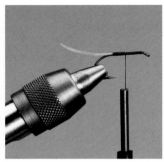

4 The bobbin is in a position to construct the body.

DUBBING

There are many different methods of forming the body of a fly. A widely practised method is to dub the fly using either natural or synthetic materials, with the most commonly used material being the fur from a hare's mask. This process involves applying material fibres to the bobbin thread to form a rope. The rope is

then wound neatly around the shank of the hook, creating the body of the fly. Some materials are difficult to dub on to a plain thread. If you have difficulty, you can use a waxed thread instead. Pre-waxed thread is available from suppliers, or you can treat plain thread with fly tyer's wax.

1 Prepare a foundation of neat touching turns down to the bend of the hook. Offer up a small pinch of the prepared fur to the bobbin thread.

2 Using the thumb and forefinger, roll the fur in one direction so that it binds to the thread, forming a rope.

3 Carefully wind the rope up and over the hook shank, moving down towards the eye in even turns.

4 Use a dubbing needle to carefully pick out fibres between the bobbin threads to create the desired effect.

TYING A HACKLE

Hackles imitate the legs of the natural insect on both dry and wet fly patterns. On a dry fly pattern the hackle is used to provide buoyancy, enabling the fly to sit in the surface film of the water. The density of the hackle determines the buoyancy of the fly, so it is important to choose the right material for each pattern

that you make. Hackles are formed using a wide range of materials, most usually feathers from a variety of genetically reared fowl; these are available in natural or dyed colours. The selection of the feather used and the area of the cape it is taken from will depend upon the type of hackle required.

1 Offer up the hackle to the head of the fly, ensuring the good side of the hackle is facing forward.

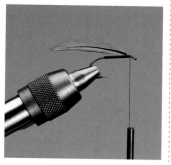

2 Secure the hackle in place with four or five turns of thread. Check that the good side of the hackle is still facing forward.

3 Carefully trap the end of the hackle in the jaws of the hackle pliers and begin to wind the hackle around the shank of the hook, towards the eye.

4 The hackle is trapped by the bobbin thread. Trim away any waste material carefully.

TYING WINGS

Wings are used either to imitate the wings of a natural insect in its emergent or adult form or to add movement to a fly. Different material is used, depending on the required effect. Of the many various materials used to construct the wings of a fly, feather fibre is among the most common and realistic.

The step sequence below shows you how to construct a wing using paired feathers or slips. These slips must be selected from two matching feathers taken from each side of the fowl. By following this basic method you can add wings to any pattern you are attempting to make.

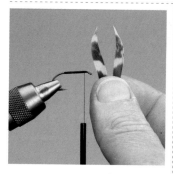

1 Select two slips that are identical in length, width and colour variations and hold them together.

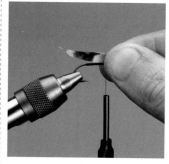

2 The slips will naturally bond together. Offer up the slips to the head of the hook above the shank.

3 Wrap the bobbin thread over the paired slips enough times to secure the wings to the hook shank. The position of the wings must remain upright. Trim any excess fibre.

4 The wing is ready to receive a hackle or a whip finish.

ADAMS DRY FLY

The Adams is probably the most popular dry fly pattern in use today. Although it imitates no particular insect, the use of mixed red game and grizzle hackles produces an impression of a natural olive, making the Adams highly effective especially during a hatch of olive duns.

HOOK	Size 12–22 light wire dry fly
THREAD	Black
TAIL	Mixed natural red game and grizzle cock hackle fibres
BODY	Muskrat or grey rabbit
HACKLE	Mixed natural red game and grizzle cock hackles
WING	Grizzle hackle points

1 Fix the hook in the vice jaws and run the thread down to the bend. Catch in natural red and grizzle cock hackle fibres at the tail. Slip one turn of the thread under the tail to cock it.

2 Select two well-marked grizzle cock hackles. They should be of equal size and with no broken fibres. Wider feathers farther up the cape are the best.

3 Having taken the thread close to the eye, strip the hackle fibres from the stems to leave two short tips. These should be slightly longer than the hook shank.

4 With the hackle tips placed together, curves apart, catch them in with the tying thread over the bare stems. Make sure that the feathers lie on top of the hook shank.

5 Lift the feather tips to the vertical. Run the tying thread around their base to secure them. Extra turns behind the tips will keep them in the correct position on the hook.

6 To ensure that the tips stay slightly apart draw the bare stems back between them and secure them along the hook shank. This also makes doubly sure that the tips stay in position.

7 Take the thread down to the tail. Dub a pinch of muskrat or grey rabbit fur to the thread using a finger-and-thumb twist. It can help to apply wax to the thread.

8 Having created a tapering rope, wind it up over the shank in close turns. Stop just short of the wings to leave room for the hackles that have to be wound on to the fly last of all.

9 Select two well-coloured cock hackles – one of natural red game, the other of grizzle. Ensure that they have the same fibre length and that they are not damaged in any way.

10 Remove any soft, downy material from the base of both hackles to leave a short section of bare stem. Use this bare section to catch in the hackles at the base of the wings.

11 Keeping both hackles together, grasp the tips with a pair of hackle pliers. Carefully, so the feathers don't separate, wind them first behind, then in front of the wings.

12 Secure the tips of the hackles at the eye before removing the waste. Build a small neat head, and then complete the fly with a whip finish and a dab of varnish.

SILVER INVICTA

The Silver Invicta, although an old and classic wet fly pattern, has stood the test of time well. This fly is regularly used by trout anglers who choose to fish, employing the traditional 'loch-style' method, from a drifting boat. It is favoured by those pursuing salmon and sea trout when river or loch fishing.

HOOK	Wet fly sproat. Size 8–14
THREAD	Black
RIB	Medium silver wire
TAIL	Golden pheasant crest
BODY	Flat silver tinsel
HACKLE	Red game cock
FALSE HACKLE	Blue jay
WING	Paired hen pheasant slips

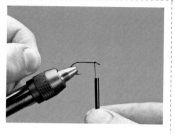

1 Tie on the thread, then neatly tie in a length of silver wire. Take the thread in neat, touching turns down to the bend of the hook.

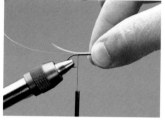

2 For the tail, select a bunch of golden pheasant crest. Position the fibres on top of the hook, then tie in at the bend of the hook. Trim any waste material.

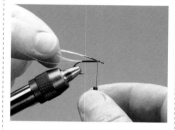

3 Take the thread in neat, touching turns back towards the eye of the hook.

4 To form the body, offer up a length of silver tinsel. Tie it in and wind it back to the bend of the hook in close, touching turns.

5 Bring the tinsel back down the hook, forming a neat and flat double layer. Tie off the tinsel at the head near the eye of the hook and trim any waste.

6 For the hackle, tie in a prepared red game cock hackle, as shown.

7 Clamp the tip of the hackle in the jaws of the hackle pliers and wind the hackle in even turns down to the bend of the hook.

8 Take the silver wire up and over the shank of the hook, trapping the tip of the cock hackle.

9 With the silver wire, rib the body in neat turns back to the eye of the hook, trapping it in place with a few firm turns of thread. Trim off any excess wire.

10 To construct the false hackle, tie in a bunch of blue jay feather fibres so that they sit on the underside of the hook shank. Secure in place and trim any waste.

11 Tie in the paired wing slips, making sure that they are secure and sit upright on top of the shank.

12 Trim the wing and form a neat head of thread. Tie off with a whip finish and varnish the head.

CAT'S WHISKER

This lure takes its name from the white cats' whiskers that were originally used in tying this pattern. The modern-day version of this fly is tied with commercially available materials. The pattern is an attractor, with its allure being its colour combination and mobility.

HOOK	Long shank lure/streamer. Size 6–10
THREAD	Glo-brite fluorescent yellow
TAIL/WING	White marabou
BODY	Fluorescent yellow chenille
OVERWING	Six strands medium, flat silver tinsel
EYES	Jungle cock

1 Tie on, then take the thread in touching turns down to the bend of the hook. For the body, reveal the core of the chenille at one end and tie in.

2 Select a bunch of white marabou fibres and offer them up to the hook. The waste materials should be the same length as the intended body.

3 Secure the marabou tail to the top of the hook shank with a few tight turns of thread.

4 Wind the thread down the hook shank towards the eye of the hook, binding in the waste marabou to form an even underbody.

5 When you are satisfied with the length of the underbody, trim any waste marabou.

6 Take the chenille up and over the hook shank in touching turns back towards the eye of the hook.

7 Strip the chenille to the core and tie off the thread to form a neat finish.

8 Select and tie in a bunch of white marabou to form the wing. This should be one and a half times the length of the tail material.

9 Position the wings and secure them firmly to the top of the hook shank. Trim any waste.

10 To add to the fly's allure, tie in six strands of flat silver tinsel as an overwing. Tie in matching jungle cock eyes on both sides of the fly.

11 Trim any waste.

12 Build up a head using the thread and tie off. Varnish the head to finish.

FUZZY BUZZER

There are many variations of this buzzer, which is tied to represent the Chironomidae. The art to fishing this midge pattern is in the way that it is retrieved. When the trout are taking pupae before they emerge into their adult form, a slow figure-of-eight retrieve with the Fuzzy Buzzer can bring great rewards.

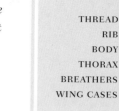

HOOK	Curved nymph. Size 8–16
THREAD	Black
RIB	Medium silver wire
BODY	Black marabou
THORAX	Black marabou
BREATHERS	White antron
WING CASES	Pheasant tail fibre

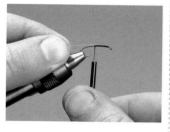

1 Tie on. Take the thread in neat, touching turns to a point halfway along the shank of the hook. Tie in a length of silver wire for the rib.

2 Wind the thread down the hook to a point just past the bend. For the body, prepare a rope of black marabou fibres.

3 Dub the body in neat, touching turns back down the shank, stopping short of the eye of the hook.

4 Rib the body with the silver wire, bringing it back over the marabou in neatly spaced turns. This will give a segmented look to the body.

5 Tie off the rib and trim any waste wire. Tie in a length of white antron at the eye of the hook, on top of the shank. Bind with a figure-of-eight weave.

6 Neatly wind the thread back to the beginning of the body.

7 Tie in two equal-length slips of pheasant tail fibre on each side of the shank. Secure. Trim any waste. Wind the thread to a point just short of the antron.

8 Prepare a rope of black marabou fibres for dubbing the thorax.

9 Dub the thorax to meet the pheasant tail slips, then back up the shank to the starting point. Fold the slips over the thorax and tie in to form the wing cases.

10 Secure the wing cases with a few tight turns of thread. Trim any waste pheasant tail fibre. Build up a neat head using the thread and whip finish.

11 Holding the two lengths of white antron tightly together with your fingers, trim them to leave enough material to represent the breathing filaments.

12 To flare the breathing filaments, use a dubbing needle to tease out the thorax and body fibres to create a life-like effect.

PHEASANT TAIL NYMPH

The Pheasant Tail Nymph is used by trout fishermen to imitate a variety of natural insects in their nymph stage. The main materials are taken from the tail of the cock pheasant. For the thorax any of the following will suffice: hare's fur, seal's fur, tinsel and most synthetics.

HOOK	Nymph. Size 6–14
THREAD	Black
RIB	Medium copper wire
TAIL	Cock pheasant tail centres
BODY	Cock pheasant tail centres
THORAX	Hare's fur
THORAX COVER	Cock pheasant tail centres
BEARD HACKLE	Cock pheasant tail centres

1 Tie on. Position the copper wire rib along the side of the hook shank. Bind in place with two tight turns of thread.

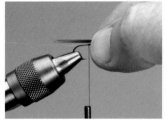

2 For the tail, prepare a bunch of pheasant tail fibres and offer them up to the hook. Place the fibres on top of the hook.

3 In neat, touching turns, take the thread down to a point just short of the hook bend. Trim any waste.

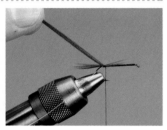

4 For the body, prepare a slip from the centre fibres of a pheasant's tail. Select the slip from the widest part of the feather to ensure enough length for body construction.

5 Wind the bobbin thread over the waste cock hackle fibres to the end of the body. Wind the fibres down the shank. Tie off.

6 Take the rib in even, open turns down the body to meet the bobbin thread. Trap the rib and trim any waste.

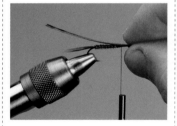

7 Select another slip of pheasant tail centre fibres and offer them up to the hook so they sit flat on the top of the hook shank.

8 Tie in the pheasant tail fibres so that they start where the body material ends. Prepare a rope of hare's fur to dub the thorax.

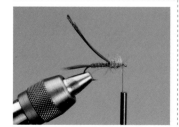

9 Construct the thorax in two or three layers. Finish with the bobbin thread just short of the eye of the hook.

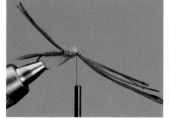

10 For the beard hackle, select another bunch of pheasant tail fibres. Tie in just behind the eye of the hook on the underside of the shank.

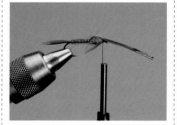

11 Trim any waste and fold the thorax cover over the hare's fur thorax. Tie in with a few tight turns of thread.

12 Trim and form a neat head using the thread. Pick out the hare's-fur fibres with a dubbing needle to form a straggly, leggy thorax. Tie off and varnish.

DEER HAIR FRY

This successful pattern can be made to imitate any number of species of small fry upon which trout avidly feed. Deer hair is used in the construction of this pattern because of its buoyant properties. The fly is fished on the surface of the water.

HOOK	Lure or streamer. Size 2–8
THREAD	Strong kevlar or equivalent
TAIL	White Arctic fox fur
BODY	White deer belly hair
EYES	Artificial adhesive eyes
COLOURING	Felt pen

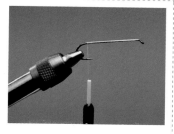

1 Tie on the thread at the eye and wind it down to the bend of the hook in neat, touching turns.

2 For the tail, tie on a bunch of fox fur at the bend of the hook with a couple of tight turns of thread to hold the material on top of the shank. Trim any waste.

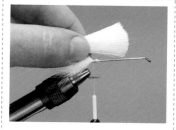

3 For the body, select a bunch of deer hair and position it on top of the hook shank.

4 Take the bobbin thread up and over the deer hair, catching it tightly on the shank at a central point.

5 Pull the thread tight allowing the deer hair to flare out and spin around the hook shank.

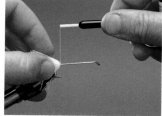

6 Wind the thread through the flared deer hair to a point forward of the bunch. Keep the thread tight. Fold the hair back towards the tail. Secure.

7 Repeat, spinning bunches of deer hair until you reach a point just short of the eye of the hook. The more deer hair you spin, the more dense the body will be.

8 Tie off with a whip finish. Remove the hook from the vice.

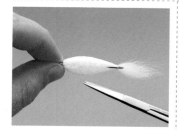

9 Carefully clip the body into shape without catching the tail material.

10 Trim the threads close to the underside of the body. This will ensure a good hook hold (the hook lies vertically when the fry is being fished).

11 Decorate the fry by applying adhesive eyes, and colour using marker pens to simulate the species of fry being imitated.

12 Varnish the eyes and head with clear varnish.

HOTSPOT LEADED SHRIMP FLY

This fly is widely used in the pursuit of trout and grayling. Its bug-like appearance and added colour attraction make this an irresistible deceiver.

HOOK	Shrimp. Size 10–14
THREAD	Black
RIB	Medium silver wire
FEELERS	English partridge
BACK	Pearl shellback
UNDERBODY	Lead wire
HOTSPOT	Red wool
BODY	Hare's fur

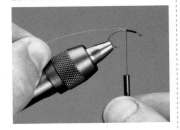

1 Tie on, then offer up a length of rib wire to the side of the shank. Tie in the rib wire and take the thread in neat turns down to the bend of the hook.

2 Neatly tie in a small bunch of English partridge fibres to represent the rear feelers.

3 Cut a strip of pearl shellback, forming a point in the material at one end to ease the tying-in process.

4 Tie in the shellback so that it sits in a central position to the rear, on the top of the hook shank.

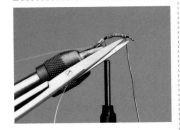

5 Taking a length of lead wire, form the underbody by winding it down the shank towards the eye in close, neat touching turns. Trim off near the eye.

6 Wind the thread up and down the shank to bind and cover the lead wire. At the eye of the hook, tie in a small bunch of partridge fibres to represent the feelers.

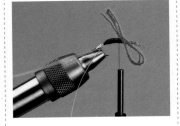

7 For the hotspot, select a length of red wool and fold it double. Tie in across the top of the hook shank using a figure-of-eight loop with the thread to secure it.

8 Take the thread back down to the bend of the hook and prepare a rope of hare's fur, ready for dubbing the body.

9 Wind on the body to imitate the curved body of a shrimp and finish with the bobbin thread at a point just short of the eye of the hook.

10 Fold the pearl shellback down over the body to the front of the hook and catch it in with a few turns of thread.

11 To form the segmented body, take the silver wire up over the shellback to the eye of the hook in open turns to form a rib.

12 Trim any waste wire and shellback. Tie off with a whip finish and varnish. Carefully trim the wool close to the body of the shrimp to form the hotspots.

SALMON SHRIMP FLY

When at sea salmon feed avidly upon shrimps, but once in fresh water and on its journey to spawn, it is in a state of fast. It is thought that salmon can still recognize the silhouette of a shrimp and will often take this pattern in an act of pure aggression.

HOOK	Salmon double. Size 4–12
THREAD	Black
BUTT	Flat silver tinsel
RIB	Medium silver wire
TAIL	Orange bucktail
BODY	Orange seal's fur
HACKLE	Orange cock hackle
UNDERWING	Grey squirrel tail
OVERWING	Golden pheasant tippets
CHEEKS	Jungle cock

1 Tie on with black thread. Take the thread in neat, touching turns to a point halfway down the hook shank. Prepare a length of flat silver tinsel and tie in.

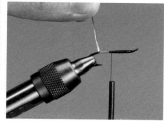

2 Wind the silver tinsel down to the bend of the hook in neat, touching turns.

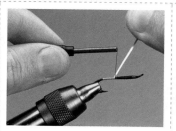

3 Wind the tinsel back over itself to the point of tying in and catch it in with a turn of thread. Trim the waste tinsel.

4 Prepare a length of silver wire for the rib and offer it up to the hook. Catch in the wire with a few turns of thread back towards the bend of the hook.

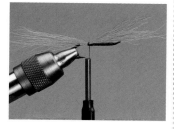

5 Select a bunch of orange bucktail and neatly tie in on the top of the hook shank. Trim any waste bucktail.

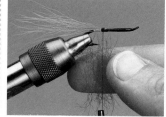

6 Prepare a rope of orange seal's fur for dubbing on to the fly's body.

7 Dub the seal's fur to the hook in neat turns to form the required body length.

8 Rib the body with the silver wire in neat, open turns and catch in with the thread. Offer up a bunch of grey squirrel's tail hair.

9 Tie in the squirrel hair on the top of the hook projecting slightly upwards. On top, tie in an overwing of golden pheasant tippets. Trim any waste.

10 Tie in a matching pair of jungle cock cheeks on each side of the body at a point just behind the eye of the hook. Trim any waste.

11 To tie in an orange cock hackle, trap the hackle in a pair of hackle pliers and wind on with three turns of the pliers. Tie off and trim any waste.

12 Build up a neat head of thread and whip finish. Varnish the head of the fly using red nail varnish.

GARRY DOG

This brightly coloured hairwing salmon fly is one of the most popular patterns and on some rivers is fished right through the year. It may be tied on a double hook or on a single or treble. The sequence shows the methods for tying a golden pheasant crest tail, a floss body, a throat hackle and the basic hairwing. These components are used in many salmon flies.

HOOK	Waddington shank. Sizes 4–10
THREAD	Black
TIP	Silver tinsel/yellow floss
TAIL	Golden pheasant topping
RIB	Oval silver tinsel
BODY	Black floss
HACKLE	Dyed-blue guinea fowl
WING	Dyed yellow hair with dyed red hair underneath

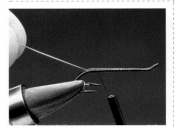

1 After fixing the hook in the vice, by one point only, run the tying thread down to a position opposite the barb. Catch in 2in (5cm) of fine round silver tinsel.

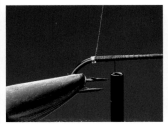

2 Take hold of the tinsel and wind it for three close-touching turns to create the tip. Secure the loose end of the tinsel with thread wraps and remove the excess.

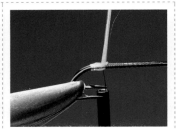

3 In front of the tip catch in 2in (5cm) of golden yellow floss. Wind on three turns ensuring each is flat and that there are no gaps. Secure the end and remove the excess.

4 Select a well-coloured golden pheasant crest feather. Choose one with a nice curve and no twists. Catch it in as a tail allowing the waste ends to lie along the shank as shown.

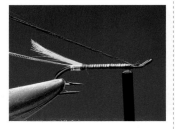

5 At the front of the tail catch in 3in (7.5cm) of silver tinsel leaving the waste end along the shank. Wind the thread to just behind the eye and catch in 6in (15cm) of black floss.

6 Take hold of the floss and wind it down the shank. Allowing the floss to flatten as it is wound will help create a smooth body. Continue winding the floss to the base of the tail.

7 Once the tail has been reached begin to wind the floss back to its catching-in point. Wind the floss so that each turn overlaps to create a tapered effect over the body.

8 Secure the loose end of the floss at the catching-in point and remove the excess. Grip the silver tinsel with hackle pliers and wind on five evenly spaced turns to make the rib.

9 Take a dyed-blue guinea fowl feather and tear off some fibres. Ensuring that the tips are level, catch the fibres in beneath the hook so that they fall just short of the hook points.

10 Remove the butts of the hackle and take a bunch of yellow hair and a smaller bunch of red hair. Place them together so that the tips are in line, red beneath yellow.

11 Estimate the wing length. It should be just longer than the hook. Cut the butts of the wing to size and catch the prepared wing on top of the shank just behind the eye.

12 Secure the hair in place with tight thread turns. Build a small head, completing with a whip finish. Finally, add a coat of black varnish to the head to finish the fly.

OLIVE GOLDHEAD

The Olive Goldhead is a deadly pattern for still water trout. The use of soft mobile marabou for the tail produces a sinuous effect in the water that trout find difficult to resist. The sequence shows how to apply a gold bead and to tie a marabou tail, a chenille body and a partridge hackle.

HOOK	Medium weight wet fly. Sizes 8–12
THREAD	Olive
TAIL	Dyed-olive marabou
RIB	Fine oval gold tinsel
BODY	Olive Chenille
UNDERBODY	Fine Lead Wire
HACKLE	Dyed-olive partridge
HEAD	3mm gold bead

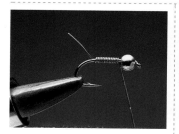

1 Before fixing the hook in the vice, slip a 3mm gold bead over the point. Push the bead up to the eye and wind on turns of fine lead wire to form a short underbody. Remove excess wire.

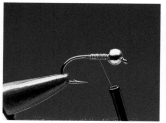

2 Run on the tying thread just behind the bead and use it to secure the lead wire in place. As a further precaution a drop of strong glue may be added to the turns of lead.

3 Take a plume of dyed-olive marabou and tear off a generous pinch of the fibres. Ensure that all the tips are in line – any that are not can simply be pinched off.

4 Run the tying thread down the shank to a point opposite the barb. Offer up the tuft of marabou, catching it in as a tail with tight turns of thread.

5 The short gap in the underbody allows the tail butts to be attached without creating bulk. That done, catch in 3in (7.5cm) of fine gold tinsel at the base of the tail.

6 Take 2in (5cm) of olive chenille. With a pair of scissors gently remove the herl from a short section of the core of the chenille. Catch the chenille in by this bare core at the tail.

7 Wind the tying thread up to the rear of the gold bead. Then, taking hold of the end of the chenille with a pair of hackle pliers, wind it, too, up to the bead in touching turns as shown.

8 Secure the loose end of the chenille with a few turns of thread before removing the excess. Wind the gold tinsel up to the bead in three or four turns up the body of the fly.

9 Select a dyed-olive, grey partridge body hackle. Choose one with fibres around twice the length of the hook gape. Make sure the feather has no broken fibres.

10 As the partridge feather has a thick stem it must be caught in by its tip. Stroke the fibre back away from the tip and catch it in just behind the gold bead.

11 Grasp the end of the partridge hackle with a pair of hackle pliers. Make only two full turns – the effect should be quite sparse. Don't wind in to the thick stem.

12 Secure the loose end of the hackle with turns of thread and remove the excess. Finally cast off the thread using a whip finish at the back of the bead to complete the fly.

KNOTS

The knots on the following pages illustrate a variety that are commonly used by coarse, sea and game anglers. Beginners should practise with string since this is easier to handle than nylon. Knots that hold the fly should be small, neatly tied and flexibile so that they move with the current of the water. Among the most *useful is the Grinner Knot, which can be tied above the eye of the hook and slid down into position. The Surgeon's Knot is used to attach droppers and join lines. The Loop Knot is ideal when you require the fly to move at the end of the tippet, and the Needle Knot is useful for tying together the fly line and leader.*

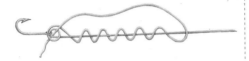

MAHSEER KNOT

This knot is well used among specimen anglers and in particular those travelling abroad. As the name suggests, it was originally used by Mahseer anglers in the giant fast-flowing Indian rivers. A good all-round knot for tying hooks to line, swivels or joining two lengths of line together.

PALOMAR KNOT

This is a popular knot for many anglers, especially carp anglers, who often use it when tying hooks on to braid rather than nylon. The knot causes the minimum strangulation and is therefore kinder to lines, particularly braid lines, which can part if too much friction is applied.

FOUR-TURN WATER KNOT

The water knot is well used by coarse, sea and game anglers and offers a good, strong, reliable knot for joining two lengths of line together. In game fishing circles it is widely used for creating droppers when fishing a team of flies, while the coarse angler will often use it to create a paternoster link.

FIVE-TURN SLIDING STOP KNOT

A stop knot can be created from heavier line or coloured power gum, to act as a marker when distance fishing. Its most common use though is as a stop when float fishing in deeper water. Tied on the line above the float at a set depth, it stops the float sliding any higher up the line.

UNI KNOT

This knot is extremely versatile and has a good following among anglers who prefer to use braided mainlines. It is used by sea anglers when the tying of large hooks to heavy-duty line is required. It is also a good knot to use with standard mono lines and offers a great strength when used for tying on hooks.

DOUBLE OR FULL BLOOD KNOT

Most commonly used for joining two lines together. A good knot for the coarse angler who needs a knot to join a lower breaking strain hooklength line to the mainline. As it is a strangulation knot it should be wetted before pulling down tight. This will help to prevent friction burns on the line.

SPADE END KNOT

Used mainly by the coarse angler, this knot is very useful for tying on spade end hooks. Although many continental anglers are able to tie tiny hooks like 24s by hand, there is in fact a gadget known as a hook tyer that will produce this knot for you in a fraction of the time it takes you to tie it.

1 Start with a 360-degree circle in the line with the loose end pointing away from the bend of the hook. The hook should lie over the line.

2 Wind the outside of the loop over the hook shank about seven to eight times. Pull the ends to tighten, and the line will be whipped into place.

SHOCK LEADER KNOT

This knot has been specially developed to join a heavy leader to a lighter mainline. It is a much-used knot for the beach angler who is casting long distances. A length of heavier line, usually 50lb (22.68kg), is joined to the mainline. This leader will then take the brunt of the cast and stop the lighter mainline from breaking.

1 Tie an overhand knot in the heavier leader and pass the lighter line through the knot alongside the protruding gap.

2 Pull the overhand knot in the leader, then wrap the tag of the mainline around the leader between six and ten times. Thread the tag back through the first wrap formed.

3 Form the knot, first with gentle pressure on the mainline against the leader, then with equal pressure as the knot closes.

4 The finished knot should be pulled firmly to ensure the 'creep' has been taken up. The tag should be trimmed.

LOCKED HALF BLOOD KNOT

This knot is used for tying on hooks or swivels to the line. It is a firm favourite among sea and coarse anglers for the joining of eyed hooks. Sea anglers often use this for tying down swivels. Being a sort of strangulation knot, it needs wetting with saliva before being tightened down, to prevent friction burn.

1 Thread the line through the eye of the hook or swivel and twist the tag and mainline together. Complete three to six twists.

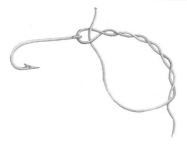

2 Thread the tag back through the first twist. The heavier the weight of the line, the fewer twists you will need to use.

3 Pull the line (but not too tightly) to begin with, so that the knot starts to form.

4 To lock the knot, thread the tag through the open loop which has formed at the top of the knot. Pull the knot up firmly and trim off the surplus tag.

DOUBLE OVERHAND LOOP

This simple but effective loop is most commonly used to accommodate a loop-to-loop hooklength. It can also be used to house a swivel or weight, by simply slipping the loop through and over the swivel or lead.

1 Form a loop at the end of your line.

2 Tie an overhand knot with the loop.

3 Add another wrap to the knot.

4 Close up the knot tightly and the loop is ready. This knot is also used when joining a cast to a mainline.

LOOP KNOT

This is a similar knot to the Grinner, and the first stages of tying the knot are the same. However, once the first overhand knot has been tied the turns are added around the mainline. This makes a good strong knot, but it is not quite as neat as some others.

1 Take the line through the hook and then tie an overhand knot.

2 Take three or four turns around the mainline above the overhand knot.

3 Pull both ends of the line to tighten the knot securely in place.

GRINNER KNOT

This knot is used by many anglers to attach the fly to the leader. It is very secure, and with practice it is easy to tie. There are a number of knots used by anglers to do this, Tucked Half Blood Knot, Turle Knot and Double Turle Knot being some of them.

1 Take the line through the eye of the hook, take it over the line and then make an overhand knot.

2 Add three or four turns to this overhand knot, depending on the thickness of the line you are using.

3 Pull both ends to tighten the knot, moistening it with saliva to prevent any line burn.

SURGEON'S KNOT

This is a good knot to use when joining two lengths of line of different strengths. It is used by sea anglers when joining a shock tippet to a mainline. The only problem with this knot is that it can be difficult to tighten properly.

1 Lay the ends of the two lines to be joined side by side. Make sure you have allowed enough line.

2 Make four overhand turns, carefully keeping the two lines as level as possible.

3 Pull steadily and slowly on all four ends to tighten the knot properly. This can be difficult.

THE NEEDLE KNOT

Needle Knots are the best way of attaching a leader to a fly line. Their main advantage is that they form a straight knotless link with the line which runs no risk of catching in the top ring of the rod. They also enable the angler to add a thick length of nylon to the fly line to assist in tapering the cast and presenting the fly more accurately to the fish. There are a number of versions of this knot, all of which are relatively easy to tie with practice. The version shown here is one of the simplest.

1 Heat a thin needle. Push the point of the needle up the core of the line.

2 Thread the nylon on the needle and push the needle out at the side.

3 Take the needle a short distance down the line and push it right through.

4 Pull the nylon through and then bring the needle back and repeat stage 3.

5 Make the second hole nearer the end of the line as shown. Thread the nylon through.

6 Tie a figure-of-eight knot at the end of the nylon to act as a stop and pull the knot tight.

A DIRECTORY OF FISHING FLIES

Now that you have explored all of the tools, materials and techniques available to the fly tyer you are ready to embark on tying your own flies from scratch. This directory is designed to allow you to explore the many beautiful flies available to you, and, with the help of the skills learned in the first half of this book, help you to tie any fly that you choose.

The directory is split into sections that distinguish the key fly types, with highly established and successful examples of each type of fly being included in each. The fly types are: dry flies, wet flies, salmon flies, sea trout flies, lures, nymphs, and buzzers. There is also a useful guide to buzzer fishing, which is a unique and relatively new way of fly fishing.

The directory gives a full materials listing for every fly, so after choosing the pattern that you want to tie you are free to embark on doing so. This will allow you to tie some truly classic flies, such as the intriguingly named Bob's Bits, the highly regarded Peter Ross, the beautiful and elaborately plumed Silver Doctor, and the much-revered Sawyer's Pheasant Tail Nymph.

There is also useful opening information to each section that explains the distinguishing features of each type of fly, and a closing glossary that explains key fly-fishing terms.

DRY FLIES

The opening section of this directory looks at a collection of some of the world's most popular dry flies. These flies are designed to float on top of the water, enticing the fish up to the surface as if they were snacking on drowning insects.

It is important to be observant and match your pattern with the insect that the fish are feeding on – the size and colour of fly are important considerations, and you should always try and match the insect hatch.

Some dry flies are designed to imitate specific insects, such as ants or mayflies, while others are more general in appearance and are intended purely to look edible – a good example of this is the Adams.

Dry fly fishing has long been regarded as the ultimate test of skill in fly-fishing circles. These small, clear waters are for the purist, who must use good judgement in selecting the right fly to tempt the quarry successfully, and who needs to be skilled in accurate casting.

ADAMS
Page 44

COACHMAN
Page 44

ROYAL COACHMAN
Page 44

BOB'S BITS
Page 45

GREENWELL'S GLORY
Page 45

PHEASANT TAIL
Page 45

WHITE MILLER
Page 46

BLUE QUILL
Page 46

COCH-Y-BONDDU
Page 46

PANAMA DRY WING
Page 47

BIVISIBLE BADGER
Page 47

MARCH BROWN
Page 47

RED ANT
Page 48

SILVER SEDGE
Page 48

CLARET SPINNER
Page 48

BLACK SEDGE
Page 49

CINNAMON SEDGE
Page 49

RED SPINNER
Page 49

BLACK MIDGE
Page 50

GREY DUSTER
Page 50

SOLDIER PALMER
Page 50

BIBIO
Page 51

OLIVE DUN
Page 51

BLACK GNAT
Page 51

BLACK SPIDER
Page 52

**GOLD RIBBED
HARE'S EAR**
Page 52

MOSQUITO DRY WING
Page 52

PROFESSOR DRY WING
Page 53

BLUE UPRIGHT
Page 53

RED TAG
Page 53

ADAMS

The Adams dry fly originates from America and was the brain child of Len Hallady, who tied the design for his close friend Charles Adams in 1922. Although the Adams imitates a wide variety of insects like duns, mayflies and midges, its origin suggests that it was in fact tied to represent a caddis, as it was first tied as a down wing fly. Since its inception it has become one of the most popular flies of all time and is extensively used all over the world.

TYING MATERIALS

HOOK
Dry fly pattern usually from 12 to 22

THREAD
Black or brown

BODY
Dubbed muskrat under fur

BODY HACKLE
Mixed grizzle and red game cock

WING
Grizzle hackle tips

TAIL
Grizzle and game cock hackle fibres

VARNISH
Clear

COACHMAN

The Coachman can be traced back to the early 1800s and attributed to Tom Bosworth, who tied the pattern as a wet fly. Tom was coachman to King George IV and his original pattern was called the Winged Brown Hackle. The Coachman dry fly is a very popular pattern among trout anglers and is a killing pattern when there are lots of Olives about. In latter years American fly tyers took the pattern further and developed The Royal Coachman, giving it a crimson body dressing.

TYING MATERIALS

HOOK
Dry fly pattern usually from 10 to 16

THREAD
Brown or black

BODY
Bronze peacock herl

HACKLE
Red game cock or ginger cock

WING
White cock hackle points

VARNISH
Clear

ROYAL COACHMAN

The Royal Coachman is regarded by the American fly tyer as the benchmark for all attractor patterns of fly, and this particular pattern is credited to American John Haily. It's a dressed-up version of the original English Coachman fly. In 1878, from his fly-tying shop in New York, Haily added a regal red band to the original Coachman pattern, making it highly desirable to the trout. It's been around now for 130 years and is an effective pattern for all-year-round use and is particularly good in coloured water.

TYING MATERIALS

HOOK
Dry fly pattern usually from 8 to 18

THREAD
Black

BODY
Peacock herl and red floss

HACKLE
Brown or red cock

WING
White duck

TAIL
Golden pheasant tippets

VARNISH
Clear

BOB'S BITS

The Bob's Bits dry fly originates from the UK and was devised by fly angler Bob Worts who is based near Grafham Water, Cambridgeshire. Bob invented the fly when he pulled 'bits' of wool from his fishing jumper to enable him to formulate a small green pattern of dry fly to imitate the small midges that the trout were taking on his local water. As it was the material from Bob's jumper that was used in the construction of the fly, the pattern was named Bob's Bits. This pattern is often tied in different-colour versions to match the hatch.

TYING MATERIALS

HOOK
Dry fly pattern usually from 10 to 16

THREAD
Black

BODY
Seal's fur

HACKLE
Game cock, very sparse on top of hook

WING
White feather fibres

VARNISH
Clear

GREENWELL'S GLORY

The Greenwell's Glory evolved from a pattern tied by clergyman Canon William Greenwell of Durham, and James Wright, a fly tyer of reputation on the Tweed in Scotland. The story goes that Greenwell asked Wright to tie up several flies of a pattern that he had devised while fishing, because the trout would not take the March Brown that he had been using. Such was the success of the new fly (taking 32 trout for Greenwell), it was named Greenwell's Glory as the fishing party celebrated later that day.

TYING MATERIALS

HOOK
Dry fly pattern usually from 10 to 16

THREAD
Primrose or yellow

BODY
Tying thread

HACKLE
Light furnace cock

RIB
Fine gold wire

WING
Blackbird or mallard/teal slips

TAIL
Optional, furnace cock hackle

VARNISH
Clear

PHEASANT TAIL

The Pheasant Tail dry fly continues to be one of the most successful patterns of dry fly to have ever been devised and is used worldwide on all manner of water for a variety of different species. Its general dowdy appearance passes it off for all manner of aquatic bug and it's a popular pattern from early April through to mid and late October. From the fly tyer's point of view it is also a very easy pattern to tie as the main bulk of material comes from a pheasant's tail.

TYING MATERIALS

HOOK
Dry fly pattern usually from 12 to 18

THREAD
Black or brown

BODY
Cock pheasant tail fibres

HACKLE
Light red cock

RIB
Fine gold wire

VARNISH
Clear

WHITE MILLER

The White Miller is a superb pattern for the evening rise as it imitates an emerging caddis that rises up to the surface during the hours of darkness. It is also often confused with a moth, and due to its colour it is highly visible from both beneath and above the surface. The wings, which are usually formed from white duck quills, are set in an upward position to the front of the shank, and a twist of either fine copper wire or silver tinsel gives it extra appeal.

TYING MATERIALS

HOOK
Dry fly pattern usually from 10 to 14

THREAD
Fine white

BODY
White floss

HACKLE
White cock

RIB
Fine silver tinsel

WING
White duck

TAIL
White hackle fibres

VARNISH
Clear

BLUE QUILL

The Blue Quill is a type of mayfly or dun pattern that offers some very good early-and late-year sport, being extremely effective for trout, even towards the back end of the winter. It boasts a body of stripped neck hackle stem and has an overall pale blue appearance. Its origin stems from the early 1900s and it is possibly a variant of the Blue Upright. The dressing allows it to stand very proud on the water, and different variations should be noted to match the hatch.

TYING MATERIALS

HOOK
Dry fly pattern usually from 14 to 18

THREAD
White or grey

BODY
Peacock quill

HACKLE
Pale blue cock

WING
Grey mallard

VARNISH
Clear

COCH-Y-BONDDU

The Coch-y-Bonddu dry fly is sometimes pronounced 'Coch-y-Bondhy' and, in fly-fishing circles, it is more commonly referred to as the 'June Bug'. The Coch-y-Bonddu hails from Wales and dates back to the 18th century; it is in fact a beetle (*Phyllopertha horticola*). It's a very good imitative pattern in mid-summer and particularly June, hence the name June Bug. When tying this pattern ensure that the body is tied with a generous amount of peacock herl – it should be nice and fat, just like the natural insect.

TYING MATERIALS

HOOK
Dry fly pattern usually from 10 to 14

THREAD
Black

BODY
Rear tag of gold tinsel, bronze peacock herl

HACKLE
Dark furnace

VARNISH
Clear

PANAMA DRY WING

The Panama Dry Wing is an attractor-type fly and is a particularly good killing pattern for brown trout. Its brightly coloured yellow silk body suggests that it was probably tied as a sea trout fly and is still very effective as such when fished in larger sizes. Its very buoyancy and fierce-looking grizzle hackle make it an extremely effective dry fly on large still water venues and rivers. Having a tail of golden pheasant tippets makes for a mosquito-type appearance that trout find irresistible. This is definitely one worth having in the fly box.

TYING MATERIALS

HOOK
Dry fly pattern usually from 12 to 16

THREAD
Black

BODY
Fine yellow silk

HACKLE
Ginger and grizzle

TAIL
Golden pheasant tippets

VARNISH
Clear

BIVISIBLE BADGER

Credit for the Bivisible Badger belongs to an American fly angler by the name of Charles Merrill, who died in 1940 and was regarded highly by the Detroit fly tyers. There are several variations of the Bivisible, another favourite being the Brown Bivisible. Created from drab brown colours, the inclusion of white, cream or silver badger to the hackle of the fly not only gives added buoyancy, but also a visible target for the angler to watch and the trout to home in on from below. A good fly to carry at all times.

TYING MATERIALS

HOOK
Dry fly pattern usually from 10 to 16

THREAD
Fine black, brown or red

BODY
Thickly palmered neck or saddle hackle in brown or grizzly

HACKLE
Silver badger

TAIL
Usually none but could add hackle fibres

VARNISH
Clear or black

MARCH BROWN

The March Brown is one of the oldest patterns of traditional dry fly in use around the world and dates back to the late 16th and early 17th century. Materials used in its construction remain little changed, although in recent years there have been several new variations of the original template for tying this pattern. It's considered a good choice when all else fails. It carries the name March Brown (*Rhithrogena germanica*), which is a creature living beneath rocks and stones which emerges between the months of February and May.

TYING MATERIALS

HOOK
Dry fly pattern usually from 10 to 16

THREAD
Dark brown or light tan

BODY
Grey rabbit or seal's fur ribbed with gold wire

HACKLE
Dark partridge

WING
Hen pheasant

TAIL
Light partridge hackle barbs

VARNISH
Clear

RED ANT

This is one of those typical traditional English patterns that demands its rightful place in the fly fisherman's fly box. A good choice for hot summer days, when the air is swarming with ants that usually end up blowing down on to the water in large numbers, with the trout waiting to intercept them. This classic pattern is very effective when tied in either red or black to simulate an ant. More modern-day patterns can be tied with the body made from foam.

TYING MATERIALS

HOOK
Dry fly pattern usually from 14 to 18

THREAD
Crimson tying silk

BODY
Crimson silk or red dubbing and bronze peacock herl

HACKLE
Natural blood red cock

VARNISH
Clear

SILVER SEDGE

The term sedge comes from the behaviour of the adult caddis fly, which can be seen clinging on to the sedge grass at the water's edge. The caddis or sedge fly has four wings, with the forward pair usually being much longer. When the wings are rested along the back of the body they give the impression of an inverted V shape. The sedge sits well on the water and is a killing pattern when there are plenty of light-coloured caddis around. Wings from the Landrail's wing feather were often used in early versions of this pattern.

TYING MATERIALS

HOOK
Dry fly pattern usually from 10 to 16

THREAD
Black

BODY
White floss

HACKLE
Ginger cock

PALMERED HACKLE
Ginger cock

RIB
Flat silver tinsel

WING
Coot

VARNISH
Clear or black

CLARET SPINNER

The Claret Spinner is a variation of the highly popular 1920s pattern the Red Spinner devised by Harry Powell, who lived in the Usk Valley, Wales. The spinner represents the second stage of a mayfly's life cycle, which trout feast on with vigour, especially when found in large numbers. Female spinners die after laying their eggs, and carpets of them can often be the doorway to a good day's fly fishing for the observant fisherman. A good pattern to carry in several different colour variations.

TYING MATERIALS

HOOK
Dry fly pattern usually from 12 to 14

THREAD
Claret or pale pink

BODY
Claret thread

HACKLE
White cock hackle

RIB
Fine flat gold tinsel

TAIL
Red hackle fibres

VARNISH
Clear

BLACK SEDGE

It is said that there are well over 300 species of sedge in the UK, and the Black Sedge dry fly can be a good choice of fly when fishing late on a summer's evening. The sedge can be tied quite large and is particularly effective on running water, its large shape making the fly splash on the water's surface as it lands. Large hatches of sedges can often be seen as early as May, particularly if it is hot, and can be evident through until October. Early sedge patterns came from Italy.

TYING MATERIALS

HOOK
Dry fly pattern usually from 8 to 12

THREAD
Black

BODY
Base of black thread

HACKLE
Palmered and shoulder hackle of black cock

WING
Black duck

VARNISH
Clear or black

CINNAMON SEDGE

Like the Silver Sedge, the Cinnamon Sedge is another good pattern of dry fly that will catch you a lot of fish when caddis are abundant and skipping across the water. One tactic that is becoming more and more popular with this pattern of fly is to twitch it violently and submerse it, allowing trapped air bubbles into the hackle and body to bring the fly back to the surface – just like its hatching counterpart. This advanced method will often bring a fast, aggressive take.

TYING MATERIALS

HOOK
Dry fly pattern usually from 10 to 14

THREAD
Brown

BODY
Cinnamon turkey herl

HACKLE
Light ginger cock

RIB
Fine gold wire

WING
Cinnamon hen or turkey

VARNISH
Clear

RED SPINNER

The Red Spinner dates back to the late 1920s and was devised by Harry Powell, who was a barber and extremely well-known fly tyer living in the Usk Valley, Wales. The spinner is the second stage of a mayfly's life cycle and has clear wings as opposed to duns. Female spinners die after laying their eggs and carpets of them can often be seen on the surface during this time. There are different spinners and the Red Spinner is that of the March Brown and Autumn Dun.

TYING MATERIALS

HOOK
Dry fly pattern usually 12 to 14

THREAD
Red silk

BODY
Red floss silk

HACKLE
Red cock hackle and blue dun near eye

RIB
Fine flat silver tinsel

TAIL
Red hackle fibres

VARNISH
Clear

BLACK MIDGE

Very similar to the Black Spider, in that it represents an extremely small item of food for the trout. Midges and chironomids are often referred to as buzzers, due to the noise they make when a swarm occurs. The adult midge is large and colourful and can usually be very evident on a warm summer evening. It often pays to check the stomach of a trout you have caught to find out the colour of midge that it is feeding on, but black is a highly favoured pattern.

TYING MATERIALS

HOOK
Dry fly pattern usually from 16 to 22

THREAD
Fine black

BODY
Black dubbing/fine silver tinsel

HACKLE
Black cock

VARNISH
Clear or black

GREY DUSTER

The Grey Duster is a favoured dry fly pattern and seems to work whatever the hatch may suggest. Being a dry pattern, it is fished on the surface film and doesn't really represent an imitation of anything in particular. Its shape and colour allow it to be seen as possibly a moth or large midge by the taking trout. The use of badger fur in the hackle makes this a very buoyant fly pattern which has proved itself to be popular on both running and still water.

TYING MATERIALS

HOOK
Dry fly pattern usually from 10 to 16

THREAD
Brown or black

BODY
Rabbit fur which is mixed with blue/grey underfur

HACKLE
Badger

TAIL
Badger hackle fibres

VARNISH
Clear

SOLDIER PALMER

The Soldier Palmer dates back to the early 1800s and was devised for fishing on the Scottish lochs where it was fished as a dropper, usually at short range. It's said that the Soldier Palmer could well have been the first ever pattern of fly specifically tied for trout. It's an attractor pattern and when fished dropper style can result in a trout bow waving towards the target with aggressive speed. It's a pattern of fly that can be used all year round but tends to give the best results from late spring to early autumn.

TYING MATERIALS

HOOK
Wet fly pattern size 10 to 14

THREAD
Black

BODY
Scarlet seal's fur or red wool

HACKLE
Palmered chestnut cock

RIB
Gold wire

BIBIO

The Bibio was the creation of Major Charles Roberts who controlled the fishing on the Burrisholle estate in Mayo, Ireland. It was tied to represent a type of heather beetle and used to catch sea trout on Lough Furnace. It's often referred to as a hawthorn fly pattern in the UK and there are many different variations including the modern-day foam versions, which will float without the need for a floatant treatment. In the United States it is referred to as the March Fly, and this is the month when it scores best.

TYING MATERIALS

HOOK
Dry fly pattern usually 12 to 14

THREAD
Black

BODY
Black cock

HACKLE
Black cock

RIB
Fine silver wire

THORAX
Black seal's fur with red spot of seal's fur

VARNISH
Clear

OLIVE DUN

Duns come in all manner of different species but are all very similar in that they are dull brown and olive in colour and form a very important part of the trout's diet. The Olive Dun is a classic trout dry fly that has been used for many years, particularly on large still waters. Late spring and summer are the best times for use, and on humid days hatching duns often take their time to leave the water, giving the trout a superb feast. It's worth carrying different shades of olive tied patterns.

TYING MATERIALS

HOOK
Dry fly pattern usually 14 to 18

THREAD
Olive or primrose

BODY
Stripped olive quill or olive dubbing

HACKLE
Olive cock fibres

WING
Grey duck or starling

TAIL
Olive hackle fibres

VARNISH
Clear

BLACK GNAT

The Black Gnat is a superb pattern of dry fly that can be used all year round but really comes into its own during the late spring through to mid-autumn. Being small, simple to tie, and representative of a tiny, black fly it's often the choice of the fly angler when all else fails. One tip that is well worth trying if the fly is being refused but fish are about, is to clip the under-hackle so that the fly sits much lower in the water.

TYING MATERIALS

HOOK
Dry fly pattern usually 10 to 22

THREAD
Black

BODY
Black rabbit or seal's fur dubbing

HACKLE
Black cock

RIB
Fine oval tinsel

WING
Grey mallard or starling

VARNISH
Clear

BLACK SPIDER

The Black Spider is accredited to W.C. Stewart and dates back to 1857. In his book entitled *The Practical Angler,* Stewart wrote of and presented patterns for the Red Spider, the Black Spider and the Dun Spider. These first patterns were very sparsely dressed and are still used all season through, as they represent a range of tasty aquatic life forms, from tiny spiders to midges. The Black Spider has been referred to in the past as being the best trout fly ever. A simple yet extremely effective pattern to carry at all times.

TYING MATERIALS

HOOK
Dry fly pattern usually 12 to 20

THREAD
Brown or black

BODY
Black silk or fine black dubbing

HACKLE
Starling feather

VARNISH
Clear

GOLD RIBBED HARE'S EAR

The Gold Ribbed Hare's Ear is one the most successful patterns of dry fly of all time. Frederic Halford was responsible for the addition of the wings in the late 1880s. It was tied to represent a dun as it disengaged from the 'nymphal shuck'. Although there are several modern-day variations in the tying materials used, the original incorporates a pale primrose tying silk and starling wing. A great choice on really humid days, especially when duns are taking their time leaving the water.

TYING MATERIALS

HOOK
Dry fly pattern usually 12 to 18

THREAD
Pale primrose or brown

BODY
Primrose or brown tying silk

HACKLE
Hare's fur dubbed on to thread

RIB
Flat gold tinsel

WING
Starling or similar

TAIL
Hare's ear fibres

VARNISH
Clear

MOSQUITO DRY WING

The Mosquito Dry Wing is another great warm weather pattern of dry fly, and one that accounts for catching its fair share of trout and grayling. The name Dry Wing comes from the fact that all mosquitos have two wings and as they emerge from the depths the wings have to dry before they can take to the air. Although a very dowdy pattern, tied correctly it's a good general fly to carry with you and can be really effective when tied to smaller hooks.

TYING MATERIALS

HOOK
Dry fly pattern usually
from 12 to 20

THREAD
Fine black

BODY
Dark and pale moose

HACKLE
Grizzle cock

WINGS
Hen hackle tips

TAIL
Cock hackle fibres

VARNISH
Clear or black

PROFESSOR DRY WING

The Professor Dry Wing dates back to 1820 and was the creation of Professor John Wilson – author, poet and editor. Wilson is probably better know as Christopher North, a name he used to write under. It is told that Wilson was out fishing one day when he ran out of flies and put together a pattern made from the petals of a buttercup. It worked and the fly is still popular today, although its body is now tied with yellow silk.

TYING MATERIALS

HOOK
Dry fly pattern usually 12 to 18

THREAD
Black

BODY
Yellow silk

HACKLE
Ginger cock

RIB
Fine flat gold tinsel

WING
Mottled grey mallard

TAIL
Long red ibis feather

VARNISH
Clear

BLUE UPRIGHT

The Blue Upright was the invention of English fly tyer R.S. Austin, who lived in Tiverton in Devon and ran a tobacconist's shop. He regularly fished the River Exe in Devon and was also responsible for the development of another pattern of fly called the Tup's Indispensable. The Blue Upright dates back to the early 1900s and is widely used when there are blue or dark olives over the water. It's a pattern of dry fly that has remained extremely popular for both rivers and lakes.

TYING MATERIALS

HOOK
Dry fly pattern usually 14 to 18

THREAD
Grey or purple

BODY
Stripped peacock herl

HACKLE
Pale blue cock

TAIL
Pale blue cock fibres

VARNISH
Clear

RED TAG

Reputed to be in the region of 160 years old, the Red Tag originated from Worcester in England and was originally called the Worcester Gem. It's an exceptional choice for the fly angler who fishes running waters, and although a good all-season pattern of dry fly, it is particularly favoured by the grayling angler between the months of November and March. When tying the Red Tag a slightly longer tag can be left and then trimmed down later to suit.

TYING MATERIALS

HOOK
Dry fly pattern usually sizes
14 to 18 (up-eyed)

THREAD
Black or brown

BODY
Peacock herl (wound on to tying
thread)

HACKLE
Natural red cock

TAIL
Red wool

VARNISH
Clear

WET FLIES

In faster-flowing, deeper waters, the fly fisher may need to turn to the wet fly to find success with his quarry. Wet flies are designed to sink and often incorporate water-absorbent materials and swept-back wings and hackles to help achieve this. They vary in make-up from simple spider patterns to more complicated tying such as the Invicta, which has a palmered body hackle and a wing. Although a number are tied to imitate specific insects, either aquatic or terrestrial, the majority are tied as attractors, or simply to suggest something alive and edible.

Old established patterns like the Kingfisher Butcher and the Black Spider have served many fly fishers well. These and others are favoured for their ability to catch. A good angler, faced with difficult water, will carry a marrow spoon so that he may examine the stomach contents of the trout. Armed with the knowledge of what the trout are feeding on, he is able to match the feed with a pattern from his box.

PETER ROSS
Page 56

MARCH BROWN
Page 56

DUNKELD
Page 56

TEAL BLUE & SILVER
Page 57

BRISTOL HOPPER BIBIO
Page 57

BLACK ZULU
Page 57

GREENWELL'S SPIDER
Page 58

BUTCHER
Page 58

KINGFISHER BUTCHER
Page 58

MALLARD & CLARET
Page 59

INVICTA
Page 59

BLACK SPIDER
Page 59

COW DUNG
Page 60

PARTRIDGE & ORANGE
Page 60

SOLDIER PALMER MUDDLER
Page 60

TUPS
Page 61

BLACK & PEACOCK SPIDER
Page 61

BLUE DUN
Page 61

STONEFLY
Page 62

TEAL & GREEN
Page 62

ALEXANDRA
Page 62

WICKHAM'S FANCY
Page 63

ALDER
Page 63

BLAE & BLACK
Page 63

SNIPE & PURPLE
Page 64

TEAL & BLACK
Page 64

WOODCOCK & MIXED
Page 64

GROUSE & CLARET
Page 65

GINGER QUILL
Page 65

FIERY BROWN
Page 65

PETER ROSS

The Peter Ross was the creation of Peter Ross from Perthshire, Scotland, who back in the 19th century took the established Teal & Red pattern of wet fly and altered it. Today it's rated highly as a point fly, when fishing a team of three flies, and scores well in broken water for wild brown trout. It is also used as an imitation perch fry, particularly when rainbow trout are taking fry. Its blend of different materials has led it to become the emblem of the United Kingdom's Fly Dressers' Guild.

TYING MATERIALS

HOOK
Wet fly pattern size 6 to 14

THREAD
Black

BODY
Front half, red wool; rear half, flat tinsel, silver

HACKLE
Black hen

RIB
Fine silver wire

WING
Teal flank feather

TAIL
Golden pheasant tippets

MARCH BROWN

The March Brown has a lot going for it as a wet fly pattern, in that when tied to perfection it is a very close imitation of the natural insect. This classic pattern is said to have been a variant of Dame Juliana Berner's Dun Fly, which first came to light in 1496. The March Brown is a true classic that catches all species of trout wherever it is used. Fly anglers in Wales in particular fish it when there are hatches of the natural March Brown (*Rhithrogena haarupi*) on the water. An essential addition to the fly box.

TYING MATERIALS

HOOK
Wet fly pattern size 12 to 14

THREAD
Brown

BODY
Yellow wool with hare's-ear dubbing

HACKLE
Brown partridge

RIB
Fine gold wire

WING
Hen pheasant wing

TAIL
Brown partridge hackle fibres

DUNKELD

The Dunkeld was first recorded in *A Book on Angling* by Francis Francis way back in 1876, and has a close connection to the River Tay in Scotland, in particular the town of Dunkeld. When first discovered, it was billed as a salmon fly, but it was later discovered that when used in smaller sizes it was a killing fly pattern for wild brown trout. It became widely used in Scotland, England and Ireland as an attractor pattern on reservoirs and continues to be an extremely popular wet fly in modern-day fly fishing.

TYING MATERIALS

HOOK
Wet fly pattern size 6 to 16

THREAD
Black

BODY
Flat gold tinsel

CHEEKS
Optional, jungle cock

HACKLE
Hot orange cock

RIB
Gold oval tinsel

WING
Bronze mallard

TAIL
Golden pheasant crest

TEAL BLUE & SILVER

The Teal Blue & Silver comes from an ever-increasing family of teal-like patterns, this being the most famous in terms of its sheer killing ability. Throughout time it has established itself as a first choice for sea trout, but in latter years, and when used in smaller sizes, it has become extremely well rated for reservoir rainbow trout and also for brown trout that are feeding on small fry. A good choice on bright sunny days and also a good boat fly. When fishing with a team of three flies, use the Teal Blue & Silver on the point.

TYING MATERIALS

HOOK
Wet fly pattern size 8 to 16

THREAD
Black

BODY
Flat silver tinsel

HACKLE
Bright blue cock

RIB
Fine silver wire

WING
Teal flank feather

TAIL
Golden pheasant tippets

BRISTOL HOPPER BIBIO

The Bristol Hopper Bibio is a variant of the highly successful Bibio fly that was created by Major Charles Roberts. It was first tied to imitate the heather beetle and its first use was as a sea trout fly. However, it has gained a reputation as a killer of rainbow and brown trout and is used in running and still water the world over. For the reservoir angler this pattern, which was devised on the Bristol reservoirs in the UK, is a good choice for a 'bob' fly, allowing it to fish in the surface film and just below the surface as a semi-wet fly, as it represents lots of different insects.

TYING MATERIALS

HOOK
Wet fly pattern size 10 to 16

THREAD
Black

BODY
Black and claret seal's-fur dubbing

HACKLE
Black cock

RIB
Pearl flashabou

LEGS
Knotted pheasant centre tail

TAG
Pearl flashabou

BLACK ZULU

The Black Zulu, or just plain Zulu as is it sometimes referred to, is another classic English wet fly pattern that was first created many centuries ago. Since its conception the pedigree of the Zulu has been diluted slightly with many different variants of the original pattern. It's a firm favourite for Scottish and Irish loch fishing and is a killer when wild brown trout are the target. It's possibly the mix of black, silver and the renowned red tag tail that make it such a popular choice. Definitely one for the avid trout fisher's fly box.

TYING MATERIALS

HOOK
Wet fly pattern size 8 to 16

THREAD
Black

BODY
Black wool or seal's fur

HACKLE
Palmered black cock

HEAD HACKLE
Optional, black cock or hen

RIB
Flat silver tinsel

TAIL
Red wool or ibis feather

GREENWELL'S SPIDER

The Greenwell's Spider has been adapted from the creation of Canon William Greenwell of Durham, England, who took his original pattern called the Greenwell's Glory to Scottish fly tyer James Wright for him to tie. The Greenwell's Spider pattern, like other 'spider' patterns, was never intended to resemble a spider and the tag of 'spider' comes from the fact that when dry, the soft hackle material looks like a spider's legs. This is an excellent fly for wild brown and rainbow trout, particularly when olives are hatching.

TYING MATERIALS

HOOK
Wet fly pattern size 14 to 16

THREAD
Black

BODY
Waxed yellow tying thread with optional peacock herl

HACKLE
Long coch-y-bonddu or long furnace hen fibres

RIB
Fine gold wire

BUTCHER

This exceptional fly was originally named the Moons Fly, and only later became the Butcher as its creator was a butcher by profession. The blue mallard in the fly's wing is supposed to represent the blue butcher's apron. As a wet fly pattern it has few equals and is a killer for wild brown trout and rainbow trout on reservoirs. It works well all through the fly-fishing season, but is particularly good in spring. Yet another classic wet fly that incorporates the tried and trusted combination of red and silver markings.

TYING MATERIALS

HOOK
Wet fly pattern size 8 to 14

THREAD
Black

BODY
Flat silver tinsel

HACKLE
Black cock

RIB
Oval silver tinsel

WING
Blue mallard

TAIL
Scarlet feather fibre

KINGFISHER BUTCHER

The Kingfisher Butcher is a progression from the Butcher that originated from a Tunbridge Well's butcher's shop, in England back in the 1800s. There have been several variants of the original Butcher pattern, the Kingfisher Butcher being just one.

It is regarded as an outstanding attractor pattern for still water brown trout and also rainbows, especially on bright sunny days, when the pattern really stands out in deep water. It's also a good choice for a point fly on a team of three flies.

TYING MATERIALS

HOOK
Wet fly pattern size 8 to 14

THREAD
Black

BODY
Flat gold tinsel

HACKLE
Hot orange cock

RIB
Fine gold tinsel or wire

WING
Blue mallard, crow wing or magpie tail

TAIL
Bright blue hackle fibres

MALLARD & CLARET

The Mallard & Claret is one of the best known and most traditional wet fly patterns, and has really stood the test of time. As a killer of trout it's hard to beat on a still water when fishing for rainbow trout, particularly when fished from a boat as a dropper on a team of flies. Fly anglers across the world also favour this pattern for early season work and it's a proven catcher of trout when the air temperature is down and when there's extra water on the river. This is a must-have addition to the fly box.

TYING MATERIALS

HOOK
Wet fly pattern size 10 to 14

THREAD
Black

BODY
Dark claret seal's fur

HACKLE
Black or brown hen at the throat

RIB
Gold oval tinsel

WING
Bronze mallard

TAIL
Golden pheasant tippets

INVICTA

There are several variants of this classic wet fly, which has been an effective fly for well over a century. The word 'invicta' appears on the English county of Kent's coat of arms and means 'unconquered' or 'untamed'. It's fair to say that this pattern of wet fly has few conquerors. It's a good choice of pattern when sedges are about and is best fished just below the surface. A thickly hackled version makes a good wake fly for fry-feeding trout, particularly overwintered rainbow trout in reservoirs.

TYING MATERIALS

HOOK
Wet fly pattern size 10 to 14

THREAD
Brown or yellow

BODY
Yellow seal's fur

HACKLE
Jay fibres

PALMERED HACKLE
Ginger cock

RIB
Gold wire

WING
Hen pheasant

TAIL
Golden pheasant crest

BLACK SPIDER

Although it bears the title Black Spider this pattern was never tied to represent a spider. The spider term comes from the action of the soft, feather-type hackle, which pulses in the water as the imitation fly is retrieved by the fly fisher. Being black in colour the Black Spider lends itself to being any one of many different black insects and is readily taken by the trout. It's an old classic pattern that has been effective on river and still water for around 175 years.

TYING MATERIALS

HOOK
Wet fly pattern size 12 to 18

THREAD
Black

BODY
Well-waxed black thread

HACKLE
Starling feather

RIB
Optional fine red wire

COW DUNG

A rather peculiar name for a wet fly pattern, but one that has been around for many years. The Cow Dung wet fly is a pattern of imitation that represents the small flies that live on cow's dung. It was said to be discovered when a fly angler stepped in a cow pat and sent a swarm of tiny flies buzzing off into the air. In 1836 fly tyer Alfred Ronald tied this pattern with yellow worsted mohair and dingy brown bear fur, spun of light brown silk to good effect. It's a pattern that can be used throughout the year.

TYING MATERIALS

HOOK
Wet fly pattern size 12 to 14

THREAD
Yellow

BODY
Peacock herl

HACKLE
Ginger reddish cock

WING
Cinnamon hen wing

PARTRIDGE & ORANGE

The Partridge & Orange is a much-celebrated, very simple pattern that has roots in the county of Yorkshire, England, where it was first tied. In 1895 it was described in T.E. Pritt's book *Yorkshire Trout Flies*, where Pritt also gave credit to earlier versions under different names. The very words 'partridge' and 'orange' suggest just how easy this pattern is to tie, namely with just two materials, unless you count the thread. Traditionally it's classed as a brown trout and grayling pattern, but is exceptionally good for large still water Rainbow trout.

TYING MATERIALS

HOOK
Wet fly pattern size 12 to 16

THREAD
Orange

BODY
Orange tying silk

HACKLE
Brown partridge

SOLDIER PALMER MUDDLER

This fly is a hybrid of two classic patterns: the Soldier Palmer, a well-known traditional loch or lake fly that imitates a sedge, and the Muddler Minnow with its deer-hair head, first tied in 1967 by Don Gapen.

The combination makes a deadly lake fly for all species and the Soldier palmer Muddler is a highly suitable top dropper fly for when there is a good wave on the water.

TYING MATERIALS

HOOK
Dry fly pattern usually 8 to 16

THREAD
Brown or yellow

HEAD
Clipped deer hair

BODY
Scarlet seal's fur with palmered cock hackle

RIB
Fine gold tinsel

TAIL
Red wool or floss

VARNISH
Clear

TUPS

The Tups, or Tups Indispensable as it is also known, was created in 1890 by R.S. Austin, who was a tobacconist from Tiverton, in Devon, England. Austin was also a part-time professional fly tyer.
After his death his daughter continued to tie the pattern, but introduced small yet significant changes, like the use of seal's fur instead of mohair. When the sun reflects on the seal's fur it's said that the Tups becomes irresistible to trout, hence it is an indispensable pattern of wet fly.

TYING MATERIALS

HOOK
Wet fly pattern size 14 to 18

THREAD
Black

BODY
Pale yellow floss and seal's fur

HACKLE
Honey dun cock

TAIL
Honey dun cock fibres

BLACK & PEACOCK SPIDER

The Black & Peacock Spider is a very popular pattern of hackled wet fly that dates back to early fly tying. It is best fished just below the surface and is reputed to imitate either a snail, beetle or caddis fly and even small stone flies.
The spider reference again comes from the movement of the hackle as the fly is retrieved. Around 40 years ago it gained much popularity among reservoir fly anglers after respected fly fisher Tom Ivens showed the true potential of this classic wet fly pattern.

TYING MATERIALS

HOOK
Wet fly pattern size 8 to 14

THREAD
Black

BODY
Bronze peacock herl

HACKLE
Black hen

BLUE DUN

The Blue Dun was first tied to imitate dark olive and iron blue duns and is mentioned in the writings of Charles Cotton back in 1676. Some say that the pattern doesn't represent any particular natural insect, as there is no such thing as a blue dun. However, the fly fisher should note that when the natural olive dun hatches, this pattern is a killing choice.
One early dressing that used yellow silk and dubbed hare's ear gave an impressive shade of olive to the fly when wet.

TYING MATERIALS

HOOK
Wet fly pattern size 12 to 18

THREAD
Grey

BODY
Dubbed muskrat underfur

HACKLE
Grey hen hackle

WINGS
Grey mallard

TAIL
Dun hackle fibres

STONEFLY

The name Stonefly is derived from the natural insect that lives in and around rocks and stones in well-oxygenated water, especially streams and rivers. There are several different colours from pale yellow and light brown, through to pale gold and pinkish. The fly fisher has recently imitated this natural insect with a dark or black pattern that is extremely ugly in appearance, but is a pattern of fly that seems to score well, particularly on rivers for brown trout and grayling.

TYING MATERIALS

HOOK
Wet fly pattern size 8 to 18

THREAD
Pale yellow

BODY
Yellow dubbing, optional lead wire

ABDOMEN
Yellow dubbing

THORAX
Yellw dubbing

RIB
Larva lace

WINGS
Woodcock

TAIL
White turkey biots

TEAL & GREEN

The Teal & Green is one of many in the Teal series of flies, all of which derived from the Teal & Red, which was the forerunner for the famous Peter Ross pattern. The green was said to be used to simulate a small shrimp, and in the early days was widely used to fish for sea trout. In the modern day this pattern and other Teal patterns are widely used on reservoirs for rainbow trout and are fished on a sunken line in deep water.

TYING MATERIALS

HOOK
Wet fly pattern size 8 to 16

THREAD
Black

BODY
Green seal's fur

HACKLE
Brown hen or cock

RIB
Silver wire

WINGS
Teal flank or breast feather

TAIL
Golden pheasant tippets

ALEXANDRA

The Alexandra is also known as the 'lady of the lake'. It was first mentioned around 1860 and was named after Princess Alexandra. Two names come to the fore as creator of this pattern and they are W.G. Turtle and Newton Stacey. However, a few say that it was Dr John Brunton, the creator of the Brunton's Fancy, who was also responsible for the Alexandra. The title of 'lady of the lake' would suggest that this is primarily a still water pattern. But it also has its place in river fishing, where it was once banned for being too effective.

TYING MATERIALS

HOOK
Wet fly pattern size 10 to 12

THREAD
Black

BODY
Flat silver tinsel

HACKLE
Black hen or cock

RIB
Oval silver tinsel

WINGS
Red ibis and peacock herl

TAIL
Red ibis or red swan fibres

WICKHAM'S FANCY

The Wickham's Fancy wet fly was created to imitate drowning flies that get trapped in the subsurface film while trying to shed their case, drifting along on the wind and being pulled under by the tow. There are two claimants on the pattern, one being Dr T.C. Wickham, who took another pattern of fly, the Cockerton, to a local tyer named Jack Hammond. It is claimed that the Wickham was then adapted from the Cockerton. The second claimant was George Correll, a tyer from Winchester, England, who claimed that he had tied the pattern for Captain John Wickham in 1884.

TYING MATERIALS

HOOK
Wet fly pattern size 10 to 16

THREAD
Brown

BODY
Flat gold tinsel

HACKLE
Light brown cock

RIB
Oval gold tinsel

WINGS
Mallard slips

TAIL
Red hackle fibres

ALDER

The Alder is a very versatile wet fly based on a natural fly that is abundant around the bank side in early spring. They hatch in the margins and dry out on the bank, returning later to the water to lay their eggs. When the trout are feeding on Alder they will take a tied version with gusto, and a day of good fishing should be on the cards. This a good pattern to fish with when stalking trout in marginal areas, near to weed, in shallow water, which can be a very exciting form of fishing.

TYING MATERIALS

HOOK
Wet fly pattern size 10 to 14

THREAD
Black

BODY
Peacock herl

HACKLE
Black cock

WINGS
Mottled turkey or brown
speckled hen

BLAE & BLACK

There is an ongoing argument as to where this pattern of wet fly originates from; some say Scotland, others say it was an old, and very reliable, Irish lough pattern. Whatever its provenance, the Blae & Black is a proven catcher of trout when used as a single fly, or indeed, as its Irish heritage would prove, as a bob fly when boat fishing. It is intended to represent chironomid midges and does well early in the season.

TYING MATERIALS

HOOK
Wet fly pattern size 6 to 16

THREAD
Black

BODY
Peacock herl or black floss

HACKLE
Black cock

RIB
Silver tinsel

WINGS
Brown speckled hen

TAIL
Golden pheasant tippets

SNIPE & PURPLE

The Snipe & Purple hails from the north of England and is well over 100 years old. Even today it is a very popular pattern, particularly among river anglers for both brown trout and grayling. The purple aspect, and the fact that it is very sparsely dressed, make this fly a great searching pattern on clear waters, and it's very effective in fast shallow areas of a river, giving the target species minimal time to make up their mind and intercept the fly. The snipe feather hackle is extremely spider-like when being retrieved.

TYING MATERIALS

HOOK
Wet fly pattern size 12 to 18

THREAD
Purple

BODY
Purple floss

HACKLE
Dark feather from a snipe's wing

TEAL & BLACK

The Teal & Black is one of many variations in the Teal series of flies, all of which originate from the Teal & Red, which was the forerunner for the famous Peter Ross pattern of wet fly. In its infancy it was widely used for sea trout but in later years has been recognized as a first rate choice of wet fly pattern, and is often used as a point fly when fishing loch-style for trout. This is yet another great teal variant that's worth having in the fly box.

TYING MATERIALS

HOOK
Wet fly pattern size 8 to 14

THREAD
Black

BODY
Black seal's fur

HACKLE
Black hen or cock

RIB
Silver oval tinsel

WINGS
Barred teal

TAIL
Golden pheasant tippets

WOODCOCK & MIXED

The Woodcock & Mixed comes from a large family of similar-type patterns, with the Woodcock & Green and the Woodcock & Yellow being two other variants that are also extremely popular. British fly anglers tend to favour this wet fly pattern, and in recent years have chosen a woodcock-based fly over the more established teal or mallard patterns. It's equally at home on still or running water and is appealing from a colour point of view when seeking rainbow trout on reservoirs. A versatile fly that has its place in the fly fisher's fly box.

TYING MATERIALS

HOOK
Wet fly pattern size 10 to 12

THREAD
Red

BODY
Top half yellow, tail end red seal's fur

HACKLE
Ginger

RIB
Fine gold wire

WINGS
Woodcock

TAIL
Golden pheasant tippets

GROUSE & CLARET

The Grouse & Claret is the most popular of the Grouse series of patterns. There are two others that demand a place in the fly box, and those are the Grouse & Purple and the Grouse & Green. The Grouse & Claret has become a good substitute for the Mallard & Claret, particularly on big waters when targeting rainbow trout. This pattern, like its cousins, is a good choice as a top dropper fly when boat fishing, but do expect harsh takes as the trout comes in for the kill.

TYING MATERIALS

HOOK
Wet fly pattern size 10 to 12

THREAD
Claret

BODY
Claret seal's fur

HACKLE
purple

RIB
Fine gold wire

WINGS
Feather from grouse tail

TAIL
Golden pheasant tippets

GINGER QUILL

The Ginger Quill came to note in the 1800s and has found favour over the years with the brown trout angler who fishes the slightly faster waters of the river. With its sparse dressing and striking, defined quill body, the trout has little time to hesitate before engulfing this pattern. It has a close associate in the Red Quill and has proved to be a killing pattern on still waters for trout sipping down hatching flies. A good choice of fly pattern when targeting trout in clear water.

TYING MATERIALS

HOOK
Wet fly pattern size 10 to 16

THREAD
Grey

BODY
Stripped peacock quill

HACKLE
Ginger cock

WINGS
Grey duck quill

TAIL
Ginger cock hackle fibres

FIERY BROWN

The Fiery Brown originates from Ireland and it is noted that this particular fly pattern was voted the best sea trout fly in Ireland in 1904. It is also said that the Fiery Brown could well be a variant of the 1700s pattern the Bright Brown, which was created by Charles Cotton. This is a truly classic lake fly that has stayed at the fore for many years and works well on all manner of water, for both rainbow trout and browns. Well worth having in the fly box.

TYING MATERIALS

HOOK
Wet fly pattern size 8 to 12

THREAD
Brown

BODY
Fiery brown seal's fur

HACKLE
Beard hackle fiery brown

RIB
Fine gold wire

WINGS
Bronze mallard

TAIL
Golden pheasant tippets

SALMON &
SEA TROUT FLIES

Salmon flies are often referred to as aggravators. This is because once in fresh water the salmon does not feed and it is said that it takes the fly purely out of aggression, with no thought of food. Many of the flies tied for salmon bear a distinct resemblance to the shrimp, a species that the salmon feeds on heavily when at sea.

Old-fashioned salmon flies were tied with many feathers as their wings. They remain objects of great beauty, but nowadays salmon flies are simpler in design and easier to tie. Many use hairwings as this gives them more life in the water. All should be tied in a variety of different sizes to cope with different water levels.

There are many famous patterns of sea trout flies to choose from, some of which are illustrated in this section. They are all fished close to the surface of the water and made of lightweight materials.

ALLY'S SHRIMP
Page 68

RUSTY RAT
Page 68

SILVER GREY
Page 68

JOCK SCOTT
Page 69

THUNDER & LIGHTNING
Page 69

SILVER DOCTOR
Page 69

GARRY DOG
Page 70

MAR LODGE
Page 70

LAPWING
Page 70

BLACKIE
Page 71

BLUE CHARM
Page 71

COLLIE DOG
Page 71

GROUSE & GREEN
Page 72

THE CARDINAL
Page 72

GOLDEN PRAWN
Page 72

THE EXECUTIONER
Page 73

BLACK PENNELL
Page 73

BLUE ZULU
Page 73

ALLY'S SHRIMP

The Ally's Shrimp originates from the highlands of Scotland and has become a world renowned pattern. It was invented in 1981 and its inventor is the famous Scottish fly tyer, and great authority on salmon, Alistair Gowans. He was said to have tied the pattern to imitate a translucent type of shrimp that he had observed in the nets of a fishing trawler. The fly has gone on to achieve the status of 'Salmon Fly of the Millennium' in the United Kingdom and is one of the most popular Atlantic-type salmon flies ever created.

TYING MATERIALS

HOOK Up-eyed salmon
THREAD Fluorescent orange
BODY Front, black floss; rear, orange floss
HACKLE Orange hen feather
RIB Silver or gold oval tinsel
BEARD Grey squirrel tail
TAG Silver oval tinsel
OVERWING Golden pheasant tippet over grey squirrel
UNDERWING Grey squirrel
TAIL Orange bucktail with pear or micro flash strands

RUSTY RAT

The Rusty Rat is a hairwing pattern of salmon fly and is an exceptionally effective choice. It's well documented that the Rusty Rat originated in the year 1911, and was the creation of Roy Angus Thompson, thus it was christened the 'RAT'. There are several different patterns in the family of 'rats', all variants of the original tying. The Rusty Rat has become a widely used fly when fishing for steelhead in the United States and is very effective in fast water runs.

TYING MATERIALS

HOOK Up-eyed salmon
THREAD Black
BODY Rear half yellow or orange floss; front half peacock herl
HACKLE Grizzly hen hackle
WING Grey fox hair
RIB AND TAG Gold oval tinsel
TAIL Peacock swords

SILVER GREY

The Silver Grey was designed by renowned fly tyer James Wright, who lived at Sprouston on the banks of the River Tweed in Scotland. Wright took salmon fly design away from the old, drab-coloured flies with the tying of more complex and bright patterns. The inclusion of silver tinsel to the body area allowed more weight to the fly and consequently it fished deeper. The Silver Grey dates back to 1850 and has been a highly successful catcher of salmon in all manner of rivers around the world. This is a very worthy addition to the salmon angler's fly collection.

TYING MATERIALS

HOOK Up-eyed salmon
THREAD Black
HEAD Black wool
BODY Silver tinsel (flat)
THROAT Widgeon
TAG Silver twist and yellow silk
HACKLE Silver furnace
RIB Silver tinsel (oval)
SIDES Jungle cock
HORNS Blue macaw
WINGS Golden pheasant tippet strands and tail, bustard, yellow swan, gallina, blue macaw and mallard
BUTT Black herl
TAIL A topping two strands blue macaw and unbarred summer duck

JOCK SCOTT

The Jock Scott is one of the most recognizable salmon flies to have come out of the Victorian era of fly tying. In the late 1800s salmon flies were tied with the most exotic feathers, and the Jock Scott is a true example of the time. Its creator was Jock Scott, who was assistant game keeper to Lord John Scott of Kirkbank on the River Tweed. In later years young Jock gave the pattern to fishing tackle maker George Kelson, who tried the pattern and went on to catch great numbers of salmon. He consequently named the fly after its creator.

TYING MATERIALS

HOOK Up-eyed salmon

THREAD Black

HEAD Black varnish

BODY Yellow floss with black herl and toucan feathers. Black floss to rear.

THROAT Speckled guinea fowl

TAG Oval tinsel and yellow floss

HACKLE Black palmered overfloss

RIB Silver tinsel over black floss

WINGS White-tipped turkey with peacock tied over. Strands of peacock, yellow, scarlet and blue swan, bustard florican and pheasant tail, above strips of teal and barred summer duck.

BUTT Black ostrich herl

TAIL Golden pheasant and crow

THUNDER & LIGHTNING

This is an old classic that in modern times is produced in many different variations. The Thunder & Lightning is said to have been the creation of James Wright, a man who has played a major part in the development of the salmon fly as we know it today. The fly has proved to be a worldwide winner and its colour combination of orange, gold and brown is a particular favourite among salmon folk. It's often referred to as the 'Great Storm' as it fishes well when the river is rising, or when a spate of coloured water is running off.

TYING MATERIALS

HOOK Up-eyed salmon

THREAD Black

HEAD Black

BODY Ostrich herl or black floss

CHEEKS Jungle cock

TAG Oval gold tinsel & yellow floss

HACKLE Orange cock from second turn of tinsel

THROAT HACKLE Blue jay

RIB Oval tinsel gold

HORNS Blue macaw

WINGS Bronze-brown mallard

BUTT Ostrich herl, black

TAIL Golden pheasant crest

SILVER DOCTOR

The Silver Doctor is one of the finest 19th-century, fully dressed patterns of salmon fly and was very much in vogue with the Victorian gentry. This is another dressing that is attributed to James Wright. Dressed originally with exotic plumage from endangered species, the modern-day patterns are made from substitute materials, but are still as bright, and nearly as complicated to tie. The silver, blue and red colourings on this fly make it an essential addition to the fly box. The Silver Doctor is used worldwide and is very popular in England, Scotland, Norway and Canada.

TYING MATERIALS

HOOK Up-eyed salmon

THREAD Red

HEAD Scarlet wool

BODY AND RIB Silver tinsel

THROAT Widgeon

TAG Fine silver tinsel and yellow floss

HACKLE Pale blue

WINGS Tippet strands with golden pheasant tail, scarlet, blue, and yellow swan, florican, bustard, peacock wing, and light mottled turkey tail, teal and barred summer duck with bronze mallard roof

TAIL Pheasant and blue chatterer

BUTT Scarlet wool

GARRY DOG

A true classic that has been responsible for catching large numbers of salmon each and every year since it was first tied. History tells that a minister visiting a tackle shop in the 1920s was asked to donate some hair from the tail of his dog to complete a fly that was being tied. The dog was a golden retriever, apparently called 'Garry'. It has gone on to be a popular pattern, particularly in coloured water conditions. Bucktail in red and yellow or a similar type of hair is used in the dressing of modern-day versions.

TYING MATERIALS

HOOK Double or single up-eyed salmon

THREAD Black

HEAD Black or red

BODY Black floss

TAG Fine oval silver tinsel, yellow floss

COLLAR Mixed blue and black hackle

RIBBING Oval silver tinsel

WING Golden retriever hair or a sparse bunch of golden brown calf-tail or mixed yellow and red bucktail

TAIL Golden pheasant crest

MAR LODGE

The Mar Lodge was designed by John Lamont of Dee-side, Scotland in the year 1889. William Brown had recommended the colours, which incorporated the use of amherst pheasant in the wing. At that time the fly didn't have a name, and it wasn't until 1896 that the classic that we know today was embraced and constructed by Henry Gordon. He and the Duchess of Fife used it on the River Dee for their salmon fishing, and it was named after the hunting lodge on the Duchess's estate.

TYING MATERIALS

HOOK Double up-eyed salmon

THREAD Black

HEAD Black wool

BODY Flat silver tinsel with black floss

THROAT Speckled guinea fowl

TAG Oval silver tinsel

RIB Oval silver tinsel

SIDES Jungle cock

HORNS Blue macaw

WING Strips of yellow, red and blue swan; peacock wing, summer duck, grey mallard, dark mottled turkey, golden pheasant tail and topping

BUTT Black ostrich herl

TAIL Golden pheasant crest and jungle cock

LAPWING

The Lapwing was the creation of Major John Traherne, who is recognized as one of the most innovative fly tyers of all time. Traherne was a country man and besides his love of salmon fishing he also shot game birds, which gave him a plentiful supply of feathers for the tying vice. In 1883 at London's World Exhibition, Major Traherne won 'best tyer' with 18 of his salmon fly patterns. In his tying he used only natural coloured feathers and many of his flies incorporated leftover feathers from bird skins.

TYING MATERIALS

HOOK Up-eyed salmon

THREAD Black

HEAD Black herl

BODY In four sections, the first three butted with herl. First division, silver tinsel, with canary toucan. Second, topping coloured floss silk, ribbed with fine oval tinsel, and toucan. The third, orange silk with red crow. Lastly, red claret silk, ribbed

THROAT Red crow and jay feather

TAG Silver twist and green silk

CHEEKS Summer duck and jungle cock

HORNS Amherst pheasant

WINGS Enamelled thrush

BUTT Black herl

BLACKIE

The Blackie is an easy fly pattern to tie and is a good night fly for sea trout. It's also a very good choice for the early season fly fisher when fished hard on the bottom, and later in the season as a surface fished fly. It has also become a popular pattern to tie and present as a tandem, where one single hook sits behind the other (as pictured), with the forward hook being dressed with a long wing that reaches back over the rear hook. Some tyers often add a couple of extra touching turns of the silver wire at the bend of the hook for added attraction.

TYING MATERIALS

HOOK Sea trout down-eyed single size 8 to 12

THREAD Black

BODY Black seal's fur or black floss

HACKLE Black or blue cock

RIB Silver wire

WING Black squirrel

TAIL Black hackle fibres

VARNISH Clear or black

BLUE CHARM

The Blue Charm was originally a salmon fly pattern and has a strong connection with the River Dee in Scotland. Its blends of blue make it a very attractive pattern that is favoured during the summer months. Now tied in smaller hook sizes the Blue Charm has become a first-rate worldwide pattern for sea trout and is extremely popular in Canada and America. Its vivid colours make it perfect for fair weather – a bright fly for a bright day.

TYING MATERIALS

HOOK Sea trout up-eyed single or double size 8 to 12

THREAD Black

BODY Black floss

THROAT Blue hackle

TIP Fine oval silver tinsel

RIB Medium silver tinsel

WING Squirrel tail

BUTT Silver tinsel

TAIL Golden Pheasant

COLLIE DOG

The Collie Dog started life as a classic Salmon fly back in the 18th century, but as years passed it proved to a be a killer of sea trout. In the year of its origin fly fishers were just beginning to understand the benefits of using hairwing flies, and the Collie Dog was among the first. Most of the gentry of that time had working collies and the hair from the dog was used to form the wing of the fly. It's exceptionally good in very fast water, or when fished on a fast retrieve in slower, sluggish pools.

TYING MATERIALS

HOOK Sea trout up-eyed single size 6 to 12

THREAD Black

BODY gold tinsel

HACKLE Black cock

RIB Round gold tinsel

WING Black/white collie dog hair or black goat hair

TAIL Yellow bucktail

GROUSE & GREEN

The Grouse & Green is one of the best of the grouse-winged trout flies and is best fished where the primary colour of natural insects is green. It was first tied to represent a moth, and provides a large mouthful for any sea trout and larger brown trout. The Grouse & Green is similar to the Grouse & Claret and both have proven their worth when fished at night in shallower water. It is a favoured pattern worldwide and has become extremely popular in Canada and the United States in recent years. There are several variants but the original patterns are by far the best.

TYING MATERIALS

HOOK Sea trout down-eyed single size 8 to 12

THREAD Black or green

BODY Green seal's fur or black floss

HACKLE Natural red or green hen

RIB Oval gold tinsel

WING Grouse tail feather

TAIL Golden pheasant tippet

THE CARDINAL

There are two possible histories for this fly. The first is that it is named after the cardinal bird and its bright red feathers. The cardinal is now protected, and the feathers from the bird are no longer used for the tying of this pattern. Instead, dyed goose has become the standard for the wing. The second history is that the fly may have been intended to represent a cardinal's mitre. Whichever is true, this sea trout fly is an immensely popular pattern of choice for bright clear days and fast-running gin-clear water.

TYING MATERIALS

HOOK Sea trout down-eyed single size 8 to 12

THREAD Red

BODY Red floss

HACKLE Red tied as collar hackle

RIB Gold tinsel

WING Red goose feathers

TAIL Red goose feather

GOLDEN PRAWN

The Golden Prawn is tied to represent a small prawn or shrimp-like crustacean and, being bright in colour, is an easy target for a hunting sea trout. It's very popular in Scotland and Ireland and is used both day and night, particularly when fishing deeper glides and pools near to estuaries. This method of fishing targets fresh run fish that might still be keen to feed. The pattern features a hairwing (long and short tail), giving the fly an enticing shape and movement as it is retrieved.

TYING MATERIALS

HOOK Sea trout up-eyed single size 6 to 10

THREAD Black

BODY Gold flat tinsel

HACKLE Orange head hackle

RIB Oval gold tinsel

TAIL LONG Orange bucktail

TAIL SHORT Brown mixed bucktail

THE EXECUTIONER

The Executioner is a marvellous sea trout fly that is used worldwide, being a popular choice as far afield as Alaska. It has found a place in the fly box of many a sea trout fisher due to its ability to fool even the most wary of sea trout, especially when fishing in low water conditions. Intricate jungle cock cheeks tied forward of a red and silver body are the key ingredients to this killing pattern. It originates from an Atlantic salmon pattern but in later years has become a first-class sea trout fly on clear, fast waters, but is also a good night fly on shallow runs.

TYING MATERIALS

HOOK Sea trout up-eyed single or double size 8 to 12

THREAD Red

BODY Red floss with a forward of flat silver tinsel

HACKLE Black cock

TAG Fine oval silver

CHEEKS Jungle cock

RIB Silver tinsel

WING Black squirrel

TAIL Yellow cock

BLACK PENNELL

The Black Pennell was created in the 19th century by H. Cholmondeley Pennell, and has been a firm favourite for many years. It is often said that this fly was years ahead of its time, as when tied sparsely it will give some of its more modern-day contemporary chironomid patterns a run for their money when used for trout fishing. For the sea trout angler this pattern scores well when fished as a single fly in larger hook sizes, especially at night. There are several variants that have claret, green, yellow and brown bodies, all of which are worth trying.

TYING MATERIALS

HOOK Sea trout down-eyed single size 8 to 14

THREAD Black

BODY Black seal's fur

RIB Fine oval tinsel

HACKLE Black cock or hen

TAIL Golden pheasant tippets

BLUE ZULU

The Zulu range of flies, which include the black, gold and blue, are tied to imitate larva or drowned adult flies. Used as a lure on a reservoir they are extremely effective for catching winter trout. The sea trout angler has found success with this pattern, which has a considerable reputation when fished as a bob fly on a cast of three flies. The Zulu creates a wake as it skims the surface of the water on the retrieve, and it is this movement that brings the sea trout to rise and attack. A worthwhile addition to any sea trout angler's fly box.

TYING MATERIALS

HOOK Sea trout down-eyed single size 8 to 12

THREAD Black

BODY Black seal's fur or black wool

HACKLE Bright blue cock

PALMERED HACKLE Black cock

RIB Flat silver tinsel

TAIL Red Ibis feather or red wool

VARNISH Clear or black

LURES

On the big reservoirs where waters are deep, many anglers choose to fish with a deceiver fly. This style of 'lure' fishing leads the trout to believe it is chasing a smaller fish. A lure catches the attention of the fish by its shape and movement.

Although cock hackles were once the most commonly used material for tying lures, they have been almost entirely superseded by marabou. This soft, ultra-mobile feather is now used to produce the wings and tails on a large number of patterns for reservoirs and small still waters, because, combined with a weighted body or head, it provides the fly with an almost irresistible action.

Lures are bright and colourful and will catch the attention of a passing fish. They can be fished at all levels of the water and are most effective in the colder months when fished slowly across the reservoir bottom.

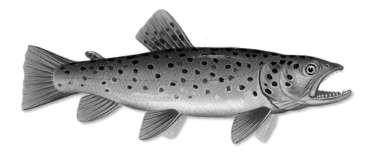

OLIVE BOOBY NYMPH
Page 76

MONTANA NYMPH
Page 76

VIVA
Page 76

JACK FROST
Page 77

WHISKEY FLY
Page 77

CAT'S WHISKER
Page 77

GOLD MUDDLER
Page 78

OLIVE DAMSEL
Page 78

OLIVE DOG NOBBLER
Page 78

ACE OF SPADES
Page 79

APPETIZER
Page 79

IDIOT PROOF NYMPH
Page 79

DAWSON'S OLIVE
Page 80

SWEENEY TODD
Page 80

ZONKER
Page 80

LEPRECHAUN
Page 81

MINKIE
Page 81

CONCRETE BOWL
Page 81

OLIVE BOOBY NYMPH

The Olive Booby Nymph was the creation of reservoir trout angler Gordon Fraser, back in the late 1970s. Gordon fished at Eyebrook reservoir in Leicestershire, England, for the large rainbow trout that were stocked there. The Booby is fished very deep on a short leader, rising when the retrieve stops, and diving when it continues. The takes from large trout are quite often very savage and strong leader material is important. The name Booby comes from the large bulbous eyes of the lure, which have been likened to a woman's breasts.

TYING MATERIALS

HOOK
Lure pattern size 6 to 10

THREAD
Black

BODY
Olive dubbing

EYES
Meshed poly balls or ethafoam

RIB
Gold tinsel

WEIGHT
Add lead wire for weight if required

TAIL
Olive marabou

MONTANA NYMPH

This particular pattern is widely used across the globe and is an imitation of a large stone fly nymph found in the western streams of the United States. It is classed as an attractor pattern and over the years it has become a very established choice on many of the stocked still waters in the UK, because of its ability to induce an aggressive take. The Montana Nymph is extremely effective when it is fished on a floating line with a long leader and retrieved very slowly.

TYING MATERIALS

HOOK
Lure pattern size 6 to 10

BODY
Black Chenille

THORAX
Yellow chenille, palmered black cock hackle finished with black chenille over the top

WEIGHT
Add lead wire for extra weight or gold bead to head

TAIL
Black cock hackle

VIVA

The Viva is a long-established pattern that has been in use on reservoirs in the United Kingdom for many years. It also scores well on newly established still water fisheries, where the stocking level is high and the trout have just been introduced. It is another example of the combination of black, green and silver, and has proved a killer pattern, particularly for big rainbow trout. It is best fished either deep and slow, or on an intermediate line slightly higher in the water column. A great addition to the fly box, especially early in the season.

TYING MATERIALS

HOOK
Lure pattern size 6 to 10

THREAD
Black

BODY
Black chenille

HACKLE
Optional, black hen

RIB
Oval silver tinsel

WING
Black marabou feather

TAIL
Yellow or green fluorescent wool

JACK FROST

The Jack Frost is another of the classic wet fly lure patterns that incorporates a killing red tag and lively marabou wing. The pattern first originated from the fly vice of the world-famous fly tyer Bob Church, who created the Jack Frost specifically for trout that were feeding on the vast shoals of bream fry at Grafham Water, England. This is an exceptional attractor pattern that works very well all through the season but really comes into its own in the early spring for over-wintered rainbow trout.

TYING MATERIALS

HOOK
Lure pattern size 6 to 10
THREAD
Black
BODY
White wool with overbody of polythene
HACKLE
Red and white mixed
WING
White marabou feather
TAIL
Red fluorescent wool

WHISKEY FLY

This hot-orange wet fly lure is a real killer during the summer months when trout are taking daphnia – a tiny animal plankton. Trout feeding on daphnia will often go mad for orange-coloured flies, and the Whiskey Fly fits the bill. It works best with quite a fast retrieve, when fished on an intermediate or normal sinking line. Let the line sink deep before starting the retrieve. This pattern was created by Albert Willock and is a killing pattern for big rainbow trout.

TYING MATERIALS

HOOK
Lure pattern size 6 to 10
THREAD
Orange or red
BODY
Hot orange thread
HACKLE
Orange cock hackle
RIB
Gold tinsel flat
WING
Orange dyed calf or squirrel

CAT'S WHISKER

The Cat's Whisker is a streamer type, wet fly lure that was created by David Train, a fly fisherman from the United Kingdom. It was aptly christened after David used white cat whiskers to hold the marabou wing in place. Like other types of wet fly lure the Cat's Whisker also comprises the essential killing combination of yellow and white, which are both highly visible to the trout, particularly fry-feeding rainbow trout. This is one of the most successful lure patterns to emerge from the British trout fishing scene.

TYING MATERIALS

HOOK
Long shank lure/streamer.
Size 6 to 10
THREAD
Glo-bright fluorescent yellow
BODY
Fluorescent yellow chenille
EYES
Jungle cock
WING
White marabou
OVERWING
Six strands medium, flat silver tinsel
TAIL
White marabou

GOLD MUDDLER

The Gold Muddler, or Muddler Minnow as it is sometimes referred to, comes from the United States and dates back to the middle of the 1950s, although clipped deer-hair patterns have been around since the Victorian age. It was tied to represent a small bullhead species found in North America and its creator was Don Gapen of the Gapen Fly Company, Minnesota. The Muddler pattern reached England in the 1960s, and was promoted heavily by Tom Saville.

TYING MATERIALS

HOOK
Lure pattern size 6 to 12

HEAD
Clipped deer hair

BODY
Gold tinsel

WING
Oak turkey

TAIL
Oak turkey

OLIVE DAMSEL

The Olive Damsel comes into its own during the month of June, especially in the United Kingdom where stillwater reservoir anglers can have some exciting sport fishing the imitation in among the natural nymph. The key to this pattern is the slim body profile and the tail movement. As with other lures the Olive Damsel is tied with a marabou tail, giving an enticing movement to the fly as it's retrieved from the depths. This is a highly successful pattern of wet fly lure, and one that the trout angler should definitely have in the fly box.

TYING MATERIALS

HOOK
Lure pattern size 6 to 12

THREAD
Olive green

BODY
Olive ostrich herl

THORAX
Seal's fur

HACKLE
Green hen

RIB
Blue wire

WING CASE
Pheasant tail

TAIL
Olive marabou

OLIVE DOG NOBBLER

The Dog Nobbler is without doubt one of the most recognized and widely used lures in the United Kingdom today. Its creator was the highly renowned Trevor Housby, an acclaimed sea angler from Hampshire in England. Trevor named his fly the Dog Nobbler because he had dubbed the large trout he was fishing for at a local water 'dogs'. The weighted head allows this lure pattern to be fished very deep, and it's a killer for large rainbow trout when tied in a variety of colours.

TYING MATERIALS

HOOK
Lure pattern size 4 to 12

THREAD
Black

HEAD
Split shot, glued and painted with eyes

BODY
Olive chenille

RIB
Silver or gold tinsel

TAIL
Olive marabou

ACE OF SPADES

The Ace of Spades wet fly lure utilizes a New Zealand-style matuka wing, capped with bronze mallard to produce a really dense profile. The Ace of Spades works well early on in the season, and should be fished very slowly along the bottom using a fast sinking line and retrieved at a slow rate with intermittent pauses. The pattern was created in the 1960s by David Collyer, a fly angler from Surrey in England, and is extremely effective in dark water. This is an excellent pattern for reservoir trout.

TYING MATERIALS

HOOK
Lure pattern size 6 to 10

THREAD
Black

BODY
Black chenille

HACKLE
Guinea fowl

RIB
Oval sliver tinsel

OVERWING
Bronze mallard strips

WING
Black hen hackles matuka style

APPETIZER

The Appetizer is another creation from the mind of the great Bob Church. It heralds from the 1970s, when Bob was pioneering English-style reservoir fly fishing, and was tied to represent small roach fry. The addition of so many colours to the tail and hackle suggests a small fry to the hunting trout. This is a great small and large trout pattern and will take both brown trout and rainbows, especially in early spring. Fish it deep or shallow and keep the fly on the move.

TYING MATERIALS

HOOK
Lure pattern size 6 to 10

THREAD
Black

BODY
White chenille

WING
White marabou overlaid with grey squirrel

RIB
Silver tinsel

TAIL AND HACKLE
Mixed green and orange cock hackle, plus silver mallard

IDIOT PROOF NYMPH

The Idiot Proof Nymph uses a soft, wavy marabou tail plus a weighted fritz body to deadly effect. It is tied in a wide range of colours, which include olive, black, pink and even orange. The Idiot Proof Nymph can be fished on either a sinking line or a floating line which incorporates a long leader. It's a pattern of lure that has proved to be very effective with highly stocked still water trout fisheries, and also demands a place in the fly box for reservoir work.

TYING MATERIALS

HOOK
Lure pattern size 6 to 10

THREAD
Pink

HEAD
Gold bead 4mm

BODY
Pink and pearl fritz

TAIL
Pink marabou and pearl flashabou

DAWSON'S OLIVE

The Dawson's Olive was created by northern England's late Brian Dawson, who was a regular at Tunstall Reservoir, Northumbria, in the late 1970s and early 1980s. As a lure, it offers the subtle combination of varying shades of olive, which gives this pattern a very natural appearance. It is possible that it may be taken as a damsel fly nymph, but Brian's pattern was tied to replicate the leeches that he found at Tunstall. When it is fished slowly on a floating or intermediate line it works on all types of still water. Watch out for takes on the drop.

TYING MATERIALS

HOOK
Lure pattern size 6 to 10

THREAD
Black

BODY
Olive chenille

HACKLE
Natural or blue guinea fowl

RIB
Silver tinsel

WING
Olive marabou

TAIL
Olive marabou

SWEENEY TODD

This pattern of trout lure is said to have been developed by the late, great Richard Walker. It's also possible that his good friend and angling companion Peter Thomas also had a hand in bringing it to recognition. The idea behind tying in the magenta colouring near the head of the fly was, it is said, to make the trout take the fly higher up the body, therefore resulting in fewer missed takes. It has been a very successful lure since its inception and is a pattern that no good trout angler should be without.

TYING MATERIALS

HOOK
Lure pattern size 6 to 14

THREAD
Black

BODY
Black floss

THROAT
Magenta wool

HACKLE
Crimson hackle fibres

RIB
Silver tinsel

WING
Black squirrel or buck tail

ZONKER

The principle behind the Zonker fly was to create a pattern that imitated small bait fish. Its roots are firmly set in America and it was conceived by fly angler Dan Byford. Dan's pattern has been widely used all over the world and tied with either natural or dyed rabbit strip. It is a killing pattern for brown and rainbow trout, particularly on big reservoirs. The fur acts as a very mobile wing when being retrieved, thus making for a great attractor pattern. The Zonker is tied in many colours, including green, black and pink.

TYING MATERIALS

HOOK
Lure pattern size 6 to 8

THREAD
Black

BODY
Grey sparkle dubbing

HACKLE
Black cock

WING
Natural rabbit strip

LEPRECHAUN

The Leprechaun pattern of trout lure was devised by fly fisherman Peter Wood and the name, not surprisingly, comes from its very bright-green colour. Since its creation in 1972 it has become a very effective pattern during bright summer days, particularly when there is a large amount of algae in the water. This is a classic trout lure that has a proven ability to attract both rainbow and brown trout to investigate its presence. This pattern is highly successful when fished slow and deep.

TYING MATERIALS

HOOK
Lure pattern size 6 to 12

THREAD
Black

BODY
Fluorescent green chenille

BEARD HACKLE
Lime green hackle fibres

RIB
Silver wire

WING
Four lime green hackle fibres

TAIL
Lime green hackle fibres

MINKIE

The Minkie was the creation of accomplished reservoir angler David Barker and it has risen through the ranks to become known as a very effective fry imitation. The pattern David devised uses a mobile strip of grey mink fur as a wing. It is at its best when fished slowly, on a sinking line, around weed beds and areas that hold shoals of small fish fry that the trout like to chase after in the summer. Vary the retrieve from slow to fast and expect fast takes.

TYING MATERIALS

HOOK
Lure pattern size 4 to 8

THREAD
Cream

BODY
Hare's-mask fur

EYES
Jungle cock

TAG
Orange wool

RIB
Silver tinsel

WING
Strip of mink fur, three times body length

CONCRETE BOWL

The Concrete Bowl trout lure was specifically devised for fishing on large manmade reservoirs and has an association with fly fisher and tyer John Gilpin, who was a regular at the Toft Newton 'concrete bowl' reservoir in Leicestershire, England. It is said that John developed this green and black pattern as a killing design for big rainbow trout on these extremely difficult waters. The Concrete Bowl can be fished in the same style as a Montana Nymph, using a long leader and floating fly line.

TYING MATERIALS

HOOK
Lure pattern size 6 to 10

THREAD
Black

BODY
Front head yellow or green chenille, back body black chenille

HACKLE
Palmered black cock hackle

RIB
Silver tinsel

TAIL
Black marabou and tinsel strands

NYMPHS &
BUZZERS

The term 'nymph' covers a larger group of patterns designed either to give the impression of something alive and potentially edible to a fish, or specifically to imitate an aquatic creature such as a shrimp. Others are tied to represent the various stages of larva, pupa or nymph which make up the life cycles of aquatic insects including damselflies and caddis flies. Many nymph patterns are tied with weighted bodies to help them sink.

Buzzers are also designed to imitate insects, specifically the midge pupa – and the term 'buzzer' derives from the sound that the natural insects make when they hover above the water. The fly is cast so that it is suspended just beneath the surface film of the water, and the fisherman then patiently waits for the fish to come and take the bait. This means that the fly has to be especially convincing, as the fish has plenty of time to examine it before deciding to take the bait.

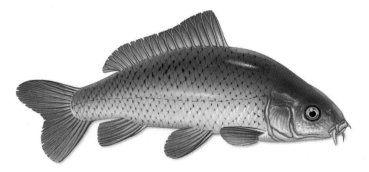

SAWYER'S PHEASANT TAIL NYMPH   *Page 84*

PHEASANT TAIL NYMPH   *Page 84*

PHEASANT TAIL SPIDER   *Page 84*

PHEASANT TAIL COVE   *Page 85*

PHEASANT TAIL ORANGE   *Page 85*

MARCH BROWN NYMPH   *Page 85*

ALDER LARVA NYMPH   *Page 86*

BROWN STONEFLY NYMPH   *Page 86*

CORIXA GOLD   *Page 86*

DIAWL BACH   *Page 87*

GREEN MONTANA NYMPH   *Page 87*

CREAM CADDIS PUPA NYMPH   *Page 87*

GREY GOOSE NYMPH   *Page 88*

DAMSEL FLY NYMPH   *Page 88*

CASED CADDIS NYMPH   *Page 88*

BLACK BUZZER   *Page 92*

SHIPHAM'S BUZZER ORANGE   *Page 92*

SUSPENDER BUZZER BLACK   *Page 92*

EPOXY BUZZER BLACK   *Page 93*

EPOXY BEAD BUZZER RED   *Page 93*

CHEW BUZZER CLARET   *Page 93*

SAWYER'S PHEASANT TAIL NYMPH

This is the original Sawyer's Nymph that has become the benchmark for all the variants that have followed over the years. Its creator, Frank Sawyer, designed this nymph from simple materials, namely pheasant tail feathers and copper wire. The amount of wire dictates the sink rate when fished on a river, and started a whole new way of fishing nymphs on running water. It is said that the copper wire that Sawyer used came from an old dynamo and the feathers from a pheasant tail, hence the name Pheasant Tail Nymph.

TYING MATERIALS

HOOK
Nymph pattern size 10 to 16

THREAD
Fine copper wire

UNDERBODY
A build up of fine copper wire

BODY
Cock pheasant tail fibres

THORAX
Cock pheasant tail fibres

WING CASE
Cock pheasant tail fibres

TAIL
Cock pheasant tail fibres, rich brown

PHEASANT TAIL NYMPH

The Pheasant Tail Nymph is a variant of Sawyer's Nymph that was originally developed by English river keeper Frank Sawyer back in the early 1950s. He devised the pattern to imitate several different insects of the baetis group which are commonly referred to as olives. Sawyer wrote two books which became world renowned and it was in his book *Nymphs & Trout,* published in 1958, that he described how to tie and fish this nymph, which has many variants today.

TYING MATERIALS

HOOK
Nymph pattern size 6 to 14

THREAD
Black

BODY
Cock pheasant tail centres

HACKLE
Beard hackle of cock pheasant tail centres

THORAX
Hare's fur

RIB
Medium copper wire

TAIL
Cock pheasant tail centres

PHEASANT TAIL SPIDER

The Pheasant Tail Spider is another variation of Sawyer's world famous nymph pattern. With its pheasant-built body the spider version of this nymph incorporates a soft hackle, which sways with a tantalizing movement as it is retrieved, tempting the trout to take without a second to think. The hackle is tied to represent moving legs and wings. This and other variants from the Pheasant Tail family have become firm favourites among trout anglers all over the world.

TYING MATERIALS

HOOK
Nymph pattern size 10 to 16

THREAD
Black

BODY
Cock pheasant tail fibres

HACKLE
Hen feather

RIB
Copper wire

TAIL
Hen feather

PHEASANT TAIL COVE

The Pheasant Tail Cove was the creation of highly respected fly fisher and fly tyer Arthur Cove, who was a pioneering still water trout angler from Wellingborough, Northamptonshire, in England. Arthur certainly had a way with nymph fishing, and his method of fishing this pattern on a very long leader and using a slow figure-of-eight retrieve was the downfall of many trout from a host of still water venues in the UK. The use of mixed seal's fur for the thorax, particularly yellow and orange, makes this nymph a classic pattern.

TYING MATERIALS

HOOK
Nymph pattern size 8 to 14

THREAD
Black or brown

BODY
Cock pheasant centre tail feathers

THORAX
Rabbit underfur or seal's-fur dubbing

RIB
Copper wire

WING CASE
Cock pheasant tail fibres

TAIL
Optional, cock pheasant fibres

PHEASANT TAIL ORANGE

Once again there's no getting away from Frank Sawyer's world-famous Pheasant Tail Nymph. In the case of the Pheasant Tail Orange, a stripped-back version of Sawyer's original pattern, all of the originality that make this a classic fly is still evident. There has been an upsurge in using different colours for the thorax for this pattern, from greens to reds and hot oranges have become popular with reservoir trout anglers, especially in the winter. As with Sawyer's original, this is an essential pattern that the keen trout angler cannot afford to be without.

TYING MATERIALS

HOOK
Nymph pattern size 12 to 18

THREAD
Black or orange

BODY
Pheasant tail fibres

UNDERBODY
Fine copper wire

THORAX
Orange silk

RIB
Copper or silver wire

WINGCASE
Cock pheasant tail fibres

TAIL
Pheasant tail fibres

MARCH BROWN NYMPH

The natural march brown nymph lives under the stones and weeds in rivers and streams. The nymph itself undergoes a two-year period underwater, where it goes through several stages of moult. They can be washed away from their underwater homes in the current, and if you are fishing an imitation it's a good ploy to fish where fast water meets calm, as this is where the trout will congregate to feed on the helpless march browns as they are washed downstream.

TYING MATERIALS

HOOK
Nymph pattern size 8 to 16

THREAD
Black

BODY
Brown floss

HACKLE
Furnace hackle

THORAX
Peacock herl

RIB
Copper wire

WING CASE
Pheasant tail

TAIL
Pheasant tail fibres

ALDER LARVA NYMPH

The alder larva nymph can be seen around the water's edge from early spring as they move into shallow water to hatch and then return to deeper water to lay eggs. The adult fly is rather large and can easily be mistaken for a caddis fly. Trout tend to ignore this in favour of the nymph. This is a good early-year pattern that can be fished in the shallows as the water begins to warm in the spring sunshine. As with other types of nymph the weighted ribbing and light underdressing of fine lead wire allows this pattern to be fished sub-surface when using a moderate retrieve rate.

TYING MATERIALS

HOOK
Nymph pattern size 8 to 12

THREAD
Black

BODY
Claret seal's fur

HACKLE
Brown partridge

THORAX
Pale white wool

RIB
Oval silver tinsel

TAIL
Cock badger tail points

BROWN STONEFLY NYMPH

Ignored in Victorian Britain, due to the popularity of dry fly fishing, the Brown Stonefly Nymph was greatly recognized by American fly fishers as a source of food for the game fish they hunted. American fly tyer's were quick to imitate this pattern of nymph that doesn't swim, instead it scurries across the bottom in search of its food.
The Stonefly sheds its skin and darkens in colour with each new coat – consequently there are several variants in colour for this pattern. Fish close to the bottom for the best results.

TYING MATERIALS

HOOK
Nymph pattern size 12 to 14

THREAD
Brown

BODY
Brown seal's fur

RIB
Brown nylon

WINGS
Mottled turkey cut into V shape

TAIL
Orange goose biots

CORIXA GOLD

The Corixa Gold is one of a number of variants for the original Corixa pattern. The late Richard Walker devised several patterns of Corixa in his lifetime, as had several other noted fly fishers. The gold version's translucent, bubble-like finish is the main attraction to the trout. Swimming up to the surface for air, the tiny Corixa dives back down with a bubble of air trapped between its legs. Corixa can be found in most large lakes and reservoirs and imitation patterns score well throughout the season.

TYING MATERIALS

HOOK
Nymph pattern size 10 to 14

THREAD
Brown or black

BODY
Flat gold lurex

BACK
Lacquered cock pheasant tail fibres

PADDLES
Two cock pheasant tail fibres

RIB
Oval gold tinsel

DIAWL BACH

The name of this nymph heralds from Wales and means 'little devil'. The original pattern was devised as a wet fly, but was later adapted to become a nymph fly. It can be fished in a variety of different ways and performs in all types of water conditions, explaining why it is one of the most popular still water flies in use today. Boat anglers catch well when using this pattern, and takes usually come when the fly is in the hang stage of the retrieve. The pattern is said to be the creation of Wyndham Davies, a Welsh International fly angler.

TYING MATERIALS

HOOK
Nymph pattern size 8 to 14

THREAD
Brown or black

BODY
Peacock herl

HACKLE
Red game cock fibres, beard style

RIB
Clear mono line

TAIL
Red game cock hackle fibres

GREEN MONTANA NYMPH

The Montana pattern is widely acclaimed around the world, and since its conception in the Rocky Mountains of the United States it has become a winning pattern on most trout waters. There are several variants, each boasting a different-coloured thorax, but green is the most popular. The pattern is tied to imitate the stonefly that lives on the bottom of fast-flowing streams and rivers, but has become a classic pattern among still water fly fishers. It is best fished on a long leader and retrieved in a slow manner.

TYING MATERIALS

HOOK
Nymph pattern size 8 to 14

THREAD
Black

BODY
Black chenille

HACKLE
Cock hackle palmered through thorax

THORAX
Yellow chenille

THORAX COVER
Black chenille

TAIL
Black hackle fibres

CREAM CADDIS PUPA NYMPH

The Caddis Pupa Nymph is an imitation of the natural caddis pupa, which can be found in abundance in most rivers and streams. It is a popular choice where caddis flies are abundant, as the trout tend to pick off the floating insects as they struggle to hatch on the surface. Cream is the most popular pattern colour for this extremely popular trout nymph. The adult fly can often be seen in the long sedge grass near to the water's edge, and this is a good indicator to the trout fisher to try the pattern.

TYING MATERIALS

HOOK
Nymph pattern size 8 to 14

THREAD
Green

HEAD
Optional gold bead for weight

BODY
Green-dyed rabbit fur dubbing

HACKLE
Hen hackle barbs

RIB
Yellow wire

GREY GOOSE NYMPH

The Grey Goose Nymph is another variant of Sawyer's Pheasant Tail Nymph, and like the original it requires a very sparse dressing to make it an effective killer for trout. The key to this particular pattern is that the thread has been replaced by a fine copper wire, which adds weight to the fly. If you intend to tie this pattern yourself look to make an exaggerated thorax, indicating that the nymph is about to hatch. Like the original Pheasant Tail Nymph, this is a fly not to go fishing without.

TYING MATERIALS

HOOK
Nymph pattern size 12 to 18

THREAD
Fine copper wire

BODY
Grey goose wing quills

THORAX
Goose feather

WINGCASE
Goose feather

TAIL
Goose feather fibres, kept short

DAMSEL FLY NYMPH

The Damsel Fly Nymph is one pattern of trout fly that every trout fisher should have in their fly wallet or box. The natural insects are a big mouthful for a trout due to their size, and in the United Kingdom there are some 17 different species. The female is a dullish green in colour while the male is more of an electric blue. The best way to fish a Damsel Fly Nymph is on a long leader with a floating line and to retrieve it in a jerky manner, almost like the real thing rising from the depths to hatch.

TYING MATERIALS

HOOK
Nymph pattern size 10 to 14

EYES
Green (optional)

THREAD
Olive green

BODY
Olive ostrich herl

HACKLE
Light green hackle

THORAX
Olive seal's fur

RIB
Medium gold wire

TAIL
Olive marabou

CASED CADDIS NYMPH

The Cased Caddis Nymph is often overlooked in the grander scheme of things, as it is quite difficult to emulate the natural insect. The caddis builds a home of sticks and stones, sticking them together to form a case. The case can often get dislodged from the river bottom, and the caddis is then at the mercy of wherever the tow takes it. Trout feed freely on caddis as they are an important food source in streams, rivers and still waters. This pattern needs to be fished deep and has an underbody of lead wire to sink it quickly.

TYING MATERIALS

HOOK
Nymph pattern size 10 to 14

THREAD
Black

HEAD
Gold bead

UNDERBODY
Fine wrap of lead wire

BODY
Dubbed hare's fur

RIB
Fine gold tinsel

TAG
Yellow

FISHING WITH BUZZERS

The use of buzzers is relatively new, as they only came to prominence in the 1960s. It is a very sedate form of fishing that sees the trout gently gobbling the fly at the end of the fly fisher's line. This means that the fish is not forced into making any rushed decisions about taking the fly, so the deception has to be even more convincing. This brief introduction to buzzer fishing covers all the basics needed for a successful day on the river.

Using a buzzer on a floating or sink-tip fly line can be a very rewarding way of catching a trout. Natural buzzers are midge pupae, and the name is derived from the buzzing sound that they make as they swarm above the water, after they have hatched. Life for the natural buzzer starts in the mud at the bottom of the lake as it is born into the world as a bloodworm, bright red in colour and resembling a tiny worm-like creature. It is the haemoglobin and oxygen held within the bloodworm's tiny body that gives it its bright red colouring, but as it matures and gets bigger the redness fades and it takes on a browny coloration. At this stage they are known as chironomid pupae. As they rise up towards the surface to hatch they become extremely vulnerable, as they are often suspended in the water columns beneath the surface film as they pause to catch their breath,

and can be picked off easily by the hungry trout. Once they reach the surface they suspend themselves from the surface film and hatch out into adult midges or buzzers. Each one of these stages can be cleverly imitated by the fly fisher, and buzzer fishing can lead to a day of highly successful fishing.

One of the first recognized patterns of buzzer can be traced back to Blagdon Reservoir in England and was created by Dr Howard Alexander Bell in the 1920s. The dressing was kept very sparse in order to mimic the tiny insect that Dr Bell was trying to imitate. That first pattern was tied using black wool, it had a silver rib, and a small plume of white wool behind the eye of the hook. This created a template for modern-day buzzer patterns, of which there are now literally thousands. It wasn't until the 1960s in England that buzzer fishing really

BELOW When buzzer fishing, it is important to have a wide variety of patterns available to you. Check the natural buzzers that are on the water and use a pattern that is similar in both size and colour.

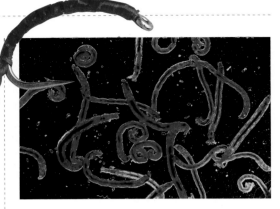

RIGHT *An Epoxy Bloodworm Buzzer designed to mimic a newly hatched bloodworm (inset).*

BELOW *Buzzer patterns are very streamlined and they use fewer materials than other, more traditional, fishing flies. Because of this they can be quite simple to tie, so are a good project for the fledgling fly tyer.*

took off, and it was the pioneering work of trout anglers such as Geoff Bucknall and John Goddard, who devised the hatching midge pupa, that helped this method of fishing to gain real recognition.

In the 1980s a pattern that was named the Suspender Midge was formulated; this buzzer was able to float in the surface film because of a small white ethafoam ball tied into the dressing at the eye of the hook. This and other patterns were the template that set many of the modern-day trends.

When fishing with buzzers the angler needs to consider several aspects, including whether to fish a single buzzer or a team of three buzzers, and the effects that the wind will have on the presentation. Teams of three buzzers work well, as they simulate part of a hatch that is about to take place, particularly when all three are fished at slightly different depths. A long monofilament leader is essential and the retrieve, if used (it is far better to fish a single buzzer on a static retrieve, just lifting the line occasionally to make the buzzer pattern rise up

from the bottom), should be in the manner of a very slow figure of eight, inducing the buzzers to lift, suspend, drop and lift again. When fishing with a team of buzzers it's well worth noting which of the team is the most effective; and if one pattern is producing and the other two aren't, then change all three to the pattern that is producing the takes.

If the trout is deceived properly, the take the angler receives will be a natural pull on the line. Buzzer-fishing takes tend to be subtle and natural, the trout literally swimming from shuck to shuck sipping them in as they move along. Once you have a take, simply tighten up the line and allow the hook to set under the pressure of the moving fish. Fine leaders should be used to imitate this sparsely dressed pattern and to allow a correct sink rate, so there's no room for a hard strike, nor is there any need with this type of fishing.

When fishing with just a single buzzer and using a static retrieve, many modern-day fly fishers employ a bite indicator (a small knot of highly visible fluorescent floss at the head of the leader), which shows any movement on the leader line. If using an indicator it is important to straighten out the fly line and leader after the cast has been made. Once fishing it's purely a case of watching for forward movement on the coloured indicator. Purist trout anglers don't tend to favour this method. Some employ a shorter leader material and prefer to watch the water at the point that the buzzer landed, actually watching the trout take it as it drops down through the water. Good eyesight and a good pair of sunglasses are essential to the success of this way of buzzer fishing.

Try to use the wind to your advantage. Buzzer activity should be evident almost every day of the year, more so in the warmer months. When looking for a place to fish, find one that provides you with a bit of a shelter from any form of rough breeze and try to get into a position where the wind is behind you. Once cast, you can speed up the drift on the leader by taking one or two steps back up the bank or slow it down by walking forward.

Single buzzers can be fished in the same manner as teams and for exceptionally wary trout a longer leader and tiny buzzer may be required. The

exception to the use of a long leader is when you find yourself casting to trout that you can see. In this case it is often better to shorten down the leader, cast to the direction in the water that the trout is swimming towards and wait for the take. If you don't have trout activity, then look at the water's surface and you might find buzzer activity or floating shucks after a recent hatch; find these and the trout won't be far away. Very often you'll

actually see the trout head and tailing, or the tell-tale dorsal fin on the surface as they gorge on midge pupa.

When it comes to size and colour choice for your chosen pattern, at the beginning of the season red works well. However, as the year wears on, darker browns, oranges and blacks are preferable. Size is also important, particularly if the trout are slightly wary. Look at the water for signs of natural buzzers and try to match what you see, in scale as well as colour. Some fly fishers will scale down to tiny size 20 or 22 hooks to get things perfectly right.

For those that want to keep their buzzers active when fishing, then an essential tip that should see you perfect the art of buzzer fishing is, if you feel the need to retrieve, do so at a rate of a metre a minute. This should see your buzzers being fished at the right depth below the surface at the right retrieve rate to simulate natural movement.

Buzzer fishing can be very exciting, and is a marked change of pace to other types of fly fishing. The deception has to be even more convincing to catch the wary, but greedy, trout – but this is ultimately one of the most rewarding ways to fish.

ABOVE *When looking for a spot to fish it is important that you find a sheltered location, as it will be much harder to control the direction of your cast if there is any wind.*

LEFT *If a trout is visible, and swimming close to the surface of the water, it is best to fish your buzzer on a shorter leader than usual and to cast towards the direction that the fish is swimming.*

BLACK BUZZER

The standard Black Buzzer has been around since the late 1920s and was brought to the attention of the trout fishing world by Dr Howard Alexander Bell, after his success with the pattern at Blagdon Reservoir in England. Being a doctor, he used to closely examine the contents of the stomach of each trout he caught, tying up imitations to replicate whatever he spooned from the gut. The black buzzer is fished on a long leader and retrieved at a very slow rate, causing it to rise and drop in the water as it moves along.

TYING MATERIALS

HOOK
Buzzer pattern size 12 to 18

THREAD
Black

BODY
Black floss

THORAX
Black floss

BREATHERS
White glo-brite

RIB
Flat silver tinsel

SHIPHAM'S BUZZER ORANGE

This pattern of buzzer was the creation of renowned fly fisher Dave Shipman, and was first tied in the late 1970s. While fishing the waters of Rutland Reservoir in England, Dave realized the need for a pattern of fly that would imitate an emerging buzzer. Dave's pattern is fished on, or near, the surface and due to the materials used it sits in the surface film, half in and half out of the water, looking like a struggling adult buzzer in hatching mode. His first pattern used a brown seal's fur, but later came reds, greens and oranges.

TYING MATERIALS

HOOK
Buzzer pattern size 10 to 16

THREAD
Orange

BODY
Orange seal's-fur dubbing

RIB
Flat gold tinsel

BREATHERS
White antron

TAIL
White antron yarn

SUSPENDER BUZZER BLACK

The Suspender Buzzer is another creation from the mind of Dave Shipman, renowned fly fisher and fly tyer. The Suspender Buzzer features an extremely buoyant polyball at the head, allowing it to sit perfectly in the surface film and mimic a hatching 'shuck'. This pattern is good in a team of flies either as the point fly or bob fly. Like other buzzer patterns it should be fished on a long leader, particularly when the trout are close in to the bank. Other than black, colours such as green, orange and yellow all work well.

TYING MATERIALS

HOOK
Buzzer pattern size 10 to 16

THREAD
Black

BODY
Black dubbing

THORAX
Peacock herl

BREATHER BUBBLE
White plastazone ball in nylon mesh

RIB
Silver tinsel

WING CASE
Black feather fibre

TAIL
White floss

EPOXY BUZZER BLACK

The Epoxy Buzzer was born out of the more traditional patterns that have emerged over many years of experimentation by innovative fly anglers. This modern buzzer pattern has many different variants and comes in a huge array of colours. The idea behind the epoxy coating is to get the fly down through the surface film quickly and to the depth at which the trout are feeding. The depth can be preset by the length of the dropper used. The Epoxy Buzzer can often bring takes on the drop, so be aware that this buzzer may invite a quick response.

TYING MATERIALS

HOOK
Buzzer pattern size 10 to 16

THREAD
Black

BODY
Black floss

OVERBODY
Epoxy resin

BREATHERS
White antron

THORAX
Black floss

RIB
Silver tinsel

EPOXY BEAD BUZZER RED

Another variation of the Epoxy Buzzer. This version features a gold bead at its head which helps to sink the buzzer deep within the water and also glints appealingly to attract any fish that are on the prowl. It can be tied in a variety of different colours, but red and orange are always successful choices towards dusk, irrespective of what colour of insect was hatching during the day. The hard epoxy finish helps to convincingly emulate the brittle exoskeleton of the natural insect, making this style of buzzer an effective choice.

TYING MATERIALS

HOOK
Buzzer pattern size 10 to 16

THREAD
Red

BEADHEAD
Copper or tungsten

BODY
Red floss

OVERBODY
Epoxy resin

BREATHERS
White antron

THORAX
Red floss

RIB
Gold tinsel

CHEW BUZZER CLARET

This buzzer was developed at Chew Valley Lake, a manmade reservoir in Somerset, and one of the United Kingdom's most revered destinations for fly fishing.

The materials used in this buzzer make it fairly buoyant and it is best fished towards the surface of the water. Claret is an effective choice of colour, but olive and black are also good options, depending on the colour of natural insect that the fish are feeding on. As with all buzzers, this should be fished on a long leader and retrieved slowly for the best results.

TYING MATERIALS

HOOK
Buzzer pattern size 10 to 16

THREAD
Claret

RIB
Silver tinsel

BODY
Claret thread

WING
White antron

TAIL
Red hackle fibres

GLOSSARY

ALEXANDRA A once-popular pattern of fly for reservoir fishing.

AMBER NYMPH Pattern of nymph created by Dr Howard Bell.

ATTRACTOR A fly pattern tied to provoke a take from a fish out of aggression.

BACKING LINE Line of dacron or monofilament used behind the fly line.

BAG LIMIT The number of fish that may be taken from a particular water.

BOBBIN HOLDER Tyer's tool used for holding the spool of thread when tying flies.

BODY Main part of the fly, covering the shank of the hook.

BREAKING STRAIN The manufacturer's estimate of the dry breaking strain of the line.

CADDIS Form of common insect.

CANE ROD Rod made from cane, a popular choice for the traditionalist.

CAPE Part of a bird skin that is used for tying flies.

CAST Action of line as it is pushed out over the water; also line used for fly leader.

CHALKSTREAM A small stream that has risen from a spring in chalk hillside.

DAMSEL NYMPH Pattern of fly very popular in modern fly fishing.

DEER HAIR Fur from a deer used for fly tying.

DROPPER Additional length of line on the leader for secondary fly.

DUBBING The use of fine fibres of material to create the body of the fly.

DUBBING NEEDLE Fine needle used to pick out fibres from a dubbed body.

DUN Type of mayfly that has just hatched on the surface of the water.

EMERGER Dry pattern of fly made to imitate a hatching insect.

FIGURE OF EIGHT The movement of the fly line in the hand as it is being retrieved.

FLOATING LINE A fly line that floats on the surface of the water.

GAPE Space between the point of the hook and the shank.

GHILLIE A person employed as a guide to anglers on salmon fishing waters.

HACKLE A cock or hen feather used to imitate the legs of a fly.

HACKLE PLIERS Fly tyer's tool for wrapping the hackle feather around the hook.

HARE'S MASK The facial area of the hare used for fly tying.

HATCH A large number of flies of the same species.

IMITATOR A fly tied to imitate the real insect.

KYPE Hooked jaw of a salmon.

LEADER Length of line holding fly below fly line.

LIE Area of the river where the fish tend to sit and wait.

LURE – Large wet fly made to imitate a small fish.

MARROW SPOON Long spoon used for inspecting the food in the trout's stomach, in order to select the right fly.

MUDDLER Commonly used pattern of reservoir fly.

NAIL KNOT A form of knot used for tying the leader to the fly line.

NYMPH Term used for insect between egg and hatching stage.

NYMPHAL SHUCK The outer layer that a dun sheds when leaving the nymph stage.

PALMERING Method employed to tie a hackle down the length of a fly.

POINT FLY Fly fished on the point of the leader when a dropper holding another fly is used.

PRIEST A small club used for the dispatching of fish.

RETRIEVE Pulling the line back in to the rod.

RISE Action of a trout as it rises for a fly on the surface of the water.

SHANK Long straight part of the hook between the eye and bend.

SPINNER A mature upwing fly.

STALKING Creeping along the bank to surprise the quarry.

STREAMER FLY An artificial wet fly with long wings, extending beyond the bend of the hook.

TAIL Part of a fly usually constructed with fine feather fibres.

TAIL FLY Same as point fly.

THORAX Part of a fly, usually constructed by dubbing.

VICE Tool used by fly tyer to hold hook while materials are tied on.

WAKE FLY Pattern of fly fished on the surface so it causes a disturbance, usually used for sea trout fishing.

WET FLY Pattern of fly fished beneath the surface of the water.

INDEX

Ace of Spades 79
Adams 26, 42, 44
aggravators 33, 66
Alder 63
Alder Larva Nymph 86
Alexandra 62
algae 81
Ally's shrimp 68
Antron 12
Appetizer 79
attractors 24, 28, 50, 54

beaded flies 13, 19
beetle 61
Bibio 51
bite indicator 90
Bivisible Badger 47
Black Buzzer 92
Black Gnat 51
Black Midge 50
Black and Peacock Spider 61
Black Pennell 73
Black Sedge 49
Black Spider 52, 54, 59
Black Zulu 57
Blackie 71
Blae and Black 63
bloodworm 89, 90
Blue Charm 71
Blue Dun 61
Blue Quill 46
Blue Upright 53
Blue Zulu 73
bob fly 57
bobbin holder 16, 17
Bob's Bits 45
body 12, 13, 24
Bright Brown 65
Bristol Hopper Bibio 57
Brown Stonefly Nymph 86
Brunton's Fancy 62
buoyancy 25, 42
Butcher 58
buzzers 44, 50, 52, 82, 89–93

caddis fly 44, 46, 48–9, 61, 82,
   86–8
Cardinal, The 72
Cased Caddis Nymph 88
Cat's Whisker 28, 77
chain 13
chenille 13
Chew Buzzer Claret 93
chironomid pupa 89
Cinnamon Sedge 49
clamp 15
Claret Spinner 48

Coachman 44
Coch-y-Bonddu 46
Collie Dog 71
Concrete Bowl 81
Corixa Gold 86
Cow Dung 60
Cream Caddis Pupa Nymph 87

damsel fly 78, 82, 88
Damsel Fly Nymph 88
daphnia 77
Dawson's Olive 80
deceivers 32, 74
Deer Hair Fry 31
Diawl Bach 87
double knot 36
double overhand loop 38
dry flies 42–53
dubbing 12, 24
dubbing needle 16
dun 44, 51, 52, 61
Dun Fly 56
Dunkeld 56

Epoxy Bead Buzzer Red 93
Epoxy Bloodworm Buzzer 90
Epoxy Buzzer Black 93
Executioner, The 73
eyes 13

feather fibre 12
feathers 10, 11, 12
Fiery Brown 65
five-turn sliding stop knot 36
flashabou 13
floss 13, 24
foams 11, 13
four-turn water knot 36
frizz fibre 13
fry 19, 31
full blood knot 36
fur 10, 11, 12, 24
Fuzzy Buzzer 29

Garry Dog 34, 70
Ginger Quill 65
gnat 51
Gold Muddler 78
Gold Ribbed Hare's Ear 52
Gold Zulu 73
Golden Prawn 72
Great Storm 69
Green Montana Nymph 87
Greenwell's Glory 45, 58
Greenwell's Spider 58
Grey Duster 50
Grey Goose Nymph 88

grinner knot 39
Grouse and Claret 65, 72
Grouse and Green 65, 72
Grouse and Purple 65
grub hook 19

hackle 25
hackle guard 16, 17
hackle pliers 16
hairwing 68, 71
head section 13
heather beetle 51
hooks 18–19
Hotspot Leaded Shrimp Fly 32

Idiot Proof Nymph 79
imitators 24, 42, 54
internet dealers 10
Invicta 54, 59

Jack Frost 77
Jay P.T. 19
Jock Scott 69
June Bug 46

Kingfisher Butcher 54, 58
knots 36–9

Lady of the Lake 62
Lapwing 70
larva 19, 73, 82, 86
lead underbody 19
lead wire 19
Leprechaun 81
lighting 14, 15
loch-style fishing 27
locked half blood knot 37
loop knot 38
lure hook 19
lures 74–81

magnifying glass 15
mahseer knot 36
Mallard and Claret 59, 65
Mar Lodge 70
marabou 24, 74
March Brown 47, 56
March Brown Nymph 85
March Fly 51
materials 10–13

mayfly 44, 48
mayfly hook 19
midge 29, 44, 50, 52
midge hook 19
Minkie 81
Montana Nymph 76, 87
Moons Fly 58
mosquito 47, 52
Mosquito Dry Wing 52
movement, adding 25
Muddler Minnow 78
mylar 13

needle knot 39
nylon thread 13
nymph hook 19
nymphs 30, 76, 79, 82–8

Olive Booby Nymph 76
Olive Damsel 78
Olive Dog Nobbler 78
Olive Dun 51
Olive Goldhead 35

palomar knot 36
Panama Dry Wing 47
Partridge and Orange 60
pet hair 11
Peter Ross 56, 62
Pheasant Tail 45
Pheasant Tail Cove 85
Pheasant Tail Nymph 30, 84
Pheasant Tail Orange 85
Pheasant Tail Spider 84
polypropylene 12
professional tuition 11
Professor Dry Wing 53
pupa 82, 87

quills 12

rayon 13
Red Ant 48
Red Quill 65
Red Spinner 49
Red Tag 53
Royal Coachman 44
Rusty Rat 68

salmon flies 66–70
Salmon Shrimp Fly 33
salmon single hook 19
Sawyer's Pheasant Tail Nymph 84
scissors 16
sea trout flies 66, 71–3
sedge fly 48, 49
sedge hook 19
Shipham's Buzzer Orange 92
shock leader knot 37
shrimp 19, 62, 66, 68, 72, 82
silhouette triggers 11, 18
silicone rubber 13
silk 13
Silver Doctor 69
Silver Grey 68
Silver Invicta 27
Silver Sedge 48
snail 61
Snipe and Purple 64
Soldier Palmer 50, 60
spade end knot 36
spider 52, 58, 59, 61, 84
spinner 48, 49
sproat hook 19
starter kits 11
stonefly 61, 62, 76, 86
Stonefly 62
storage 11, 14, 15
streamer hook 19
stretchable floss 13
surgeon's knot 39
Suspender Buzzer Black 92
Suspender Midge 90
Sweeney Todd 80
synthetic materials 10, 11, 12, 13

tail 13, 24
Teal and Black 64
Teal Blue and Silver 57
Teal and Green 62
Teal and Red 56, 64
thread 13
  bobbin holder 16, 17
  tying on 22
  waxed 13, 24
Thunder and Lightning 69
tinsel 13
tools 14–17
Tups 61
Tup's Indispensable 53

turle knot 19
tying on 22

uni knot 36

varnish 13, 16
vice 14, 15, 22
Viva 76

wax, fly tyer's 24
waxed thread 13, 24
weighted flies 13, 19, 82
wet flies 54–65
whip finish 17, 23
whip-finish tool 16, 17, 23
Whiskey Fly 77
White Miller 46
Wickham's Fancy 63
wing selector 17
wings, tying 25
Woodcock and Green 64
Woodcock and Mixed 64
Woodcock and Yellow 64
wool 13
Worcester Gem 53
worktop 14

Zonker 80
Zulu 57, 73

AUTHOR'S ACKNOWLEDGEMENTS

This book is for my dearest wife Caroline, and my children Matthew, Lucy, Luke and Beccy, all who have suffered through my infectious need to go angling... Yet again!

Sincere thanks to the team at sonicsports.com, theessentialfly.co.uk and flyfishingpoint.net

PUBLISHER'S ACKNOWLEDGEMENTS

The publisher would like to thank the following for permission to reproduce their images:
Alamy: p14 John Warburton-Lee Photography. Corbis: p6 George Obremski; p8 Dennis Wise/Science Faction; p15 Jess A. Wanskasmith/ First Light; p18 Dennis Wise/Science Faction; p20 Third Eye Images; p40 Dale C. Spartas. Getty: p90 Colin Milkins. iStockphoto: pp2; 17t; 89; 91t; 91b.